That's Very Canadian!

An Exceptionally Interesting Report
About All Things Canadian, by Rachel

VIVIEN BOWERS

ILLUSTRATED BY

DIANNE EASTMAN

MAPLE
TREE
PRESS

Maple Tree Press Inc.
51 Front Street East, Suite 200, Toronto, Ontario M5E 1B3
www.mapletreepress.com

Text © 2004 Vivien Bowers
Illustrations © 2004 Dianne Eastman

Distributed in Canada by Raincoast Books
9050 Shaughnessy Street, Vancouver, British Columbia V6P 6E5

Distributed in the United States by Publishers Group West
1700 Fourth Street, Berkeley, California 94710

We acknowledge the financial support of the Canada Council
for the Arts, the Ontario Arts Council, the Government of
Canada through the Book Publishing Industry Development
Program (BPIDP), and the Government of Ontario through the
Ontario Media Development Corporation's Book Initiative for
our publishing activities.

ONTARIO ARTS COUNCIL
CONSEIL DES ARTS DE L'ONTARIO

Dedication
For Megan and Andrew: on your marks, get set, READ!
No giggling, or Aunt Vivien will be on your case.

Cataloguing in Publication Data
Bowers, Vivien, 1951–
    That's very Canadian! : an exceptionally interesting
report about all things Canadian, by Rachel / written by
Vivien Bowers ; illustrated by Dianne Eastman.

(A Wow Canada! book)
Includes index. Ages 8–12.
ISBN 1-897066-04-X (bound).   ISBN 1-897066-05-8 (pbk.)

1. Canada—Juvenile literature.
2. Canada—Miscellanea—Juvenile literature.
3. National characteristics, Canadian—Juvenile literature.
I. Eastman, Dianne II. Title. III. Series: Wow Canada! book

FC58.B6846 2004   j971   C2004-900977-X

Design & art direction: Dianne Eastman
Illustrations: Dianne Eastman

Printed in Hong Kong

A   B   C   D   E   F

Dear Mrs. G:

Here's my report—on time! Well, actually, one day late. Please ignore the scribbles from my brother, Guy. He grabbed my report when I wasn't looking. You taught him two years ago so you know how annoying he is. Also, I accidentally left some pages on the floor and my dwarf rabbit nibbled them. The damage was pretty minor. In fact, those pages look better than the one I spilled my yogurt on. That was sure a mess before I cleaned it up.

I hope you like my report (and I get a good mark!). I learned a lot about what it means to be a Canadian. I'm guessing that's why you assigned this topic.

Your (brilliant) student,
Rachel   (just kidding)

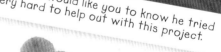

The rabbit would like you to know he tried very hard to help out with this project.

Contents

That's Very Canadian!   7

Chapter 1: Symbols That Bear the
Official Canadian Stamp of Approval   8
   Canada! Who Came Up with a Name Like That?   10
   A Buck-Toothed Beaver Becomes a National Icon   12
   Treated Like Royalty   14
   The Arms of Canada   16
   A Brisk Walk Around Ottawa, the Nation's Capital   18
   A Guided Tour of the Parliament Buildings   21
   Much Ado About the Canadian Flag   24
   How Does Canada Work?   26
   O Canada!   28
   How Will You Be Paying—Credit Card or Beaver?   30
   Loonie Toonies and Piggy Banks   32
   Branding Canada: Episode 1   34

Chapter 2: Symbols from Sea to Sea to Sea   36
   British Columbia   38
   Alberta   40
   Saskatchewan   42
   Manitoba   44
   Ontario   46
   Quebec   48
   New Brunswick   50
   Nova Scotia   52
   Prince Edward Island   54
   Newfoundland & Labrador   56
   Yukon   58
   Northwest Territories   60
   Nunavut   62
   Branding Canada: Episode 2   64

Chapter 3: Let Me Guess: You're Canadian!   66

    Hockey Night in Canada   68

    Parlez-vous Canadian?   70

    Rachel's Canadian Café   72

    Paddle Hard!   74

    We Spell It with a "U"   76

    Send in the Mounties   78

    Supersized Canada—It's Wild Out There!   80

    Meet the Neighbours   82

    Destination Canada   84

    Souvenir of Canada   86

    So You Want to be a Canadian?   88

    Branding Canada: Episode 3   90

Canuck Collage   92

Acknowledgements and Photo Credits   94

Index   95

Hi, out there. I'm Rachel and I wrote
this report with the help of my truly
Canadian team: Moose, Goose, and
Bucko Beaver.

That's Very Canadian!

I've been learning all about Canadian symbols and other things that are especially Canadian. I'm now a wiz, symbolically speaking. Watch out—you're about to find out all about these symbols, too. I'll show you all kinds of things I've found that are "Canadian," from maple leaves to words like "toque." I've also put in the things that people *think* are Canadian, even if they aren't, like that all Canadians live in igloos. As if!

Warning: One side effect of reading all this fascinating information about Canadian symbols is that you start to feel really...Canadian. Makes you want to go and paddle a canoe, or eat pancakes with maple syrup. Canada is special. For instance, what other country would have a beaver for a national symbol?

So, on with my astonishing report! Ladies and gentlemen, boys and girls, moose, geese, and beavers, turn the page to enter a country where hockey-playing beavers and maple-syrup-slurping moose live in igloos and paddle birch bark canoes in both official languages...voici le Canada!

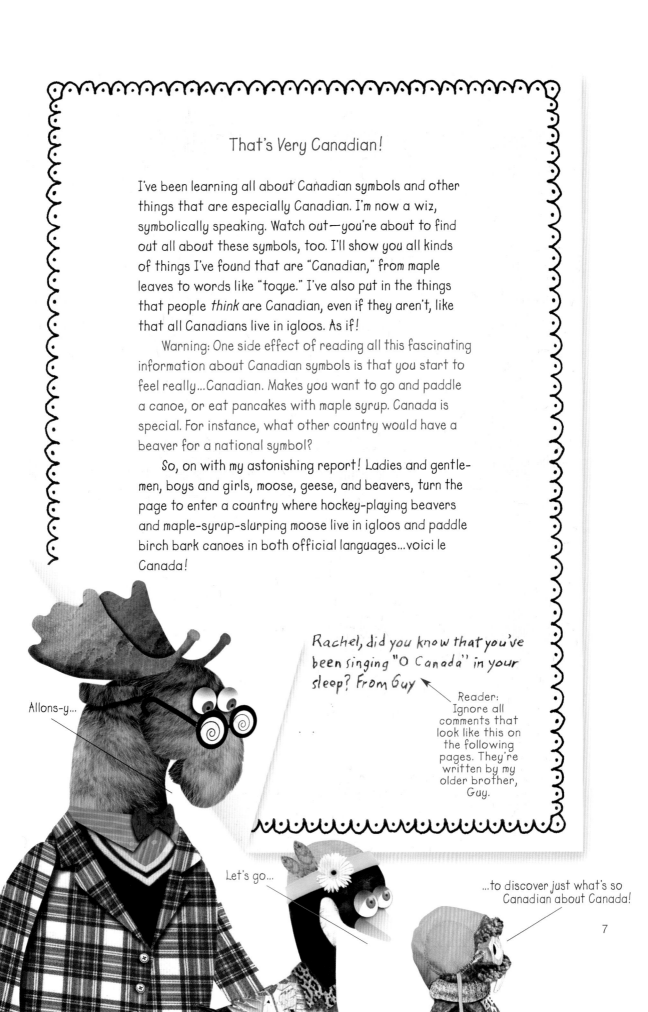

Allons-y...

Rachel, did you know that you've been singing "O Canada" in your sleep? From Guy

Reader: Ignore all comments that look like this on the following pages. They're written by my older brother, Guy.

Let's go...

...to discover just what's so Canadian about Canada!

7

CHAPTER 1

Symbols That Bear the Official Canadian Stamp of Approval

Okay, I've got the Mace, so we can get started.

I don't really need a mace to start this report. But I thought it would make things look Very Official. A mace is a big war club, but it's only ceremonial—so you'd probably never bop anyone with it. When the government is in session in the House of Commons in Ottawa, every day starts with the Sergeant-at-Arms carrying in the gold-plated Mace and putting it down on the table in the middle. The Mace is a symbol of the House's authority. Don't touch it unless you have permission.

Mine isn't exactly a gold-plated mace. I made it out of a baseball bat, an eggbeater, a trophy I got for debating in grade four, and lots of duct tape. But remember, it's symbolic. It's the idea that counts.

Besides the Mace, Canada has lots of other official stuff: flags, a national anthem, animals, coats of arms, capital cities, and symbols. But how did we end up with these things that are now "officially" Canadian? Read on to find out.

The real Mace is in Ottawa.

Canada! Who Came Up with a Name Like That?

Don't you think "Canada" is a great word? It rolls off your tongue and has a "Can do!" feeling to it. And because the word isn't English or French, it's the same in both official languages. So, we've got a great name for our country, but nobody planned it that way. Like so much else about Canada, it just...well...happened. Read on (breathlessly)!

Which Way to Kanata?

Meet Jacques Cartier, a French explorer wearing a fancy hat. In 1535, as he was sailing up the St. Lawrence River, his guides were explaining the way to Stadacona (Quebec City today). They pointed out the route to "kanata,"

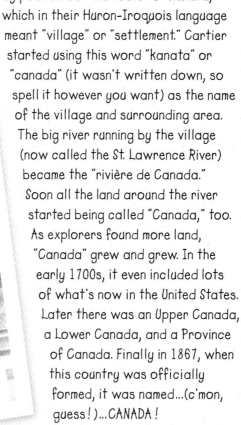

which in their Huron-Iroquois language meant "village" or "settlement." Cartier started using this word "kanata" or "canada" (it wasn't written down, so spell it however you want) as the name of the village and surrounding area. The big river running by the village (now called the St. Lawrence River) became the "rivière de Canada." Soon all the land around the river started being called "Canada," too. As explorers found more land, "Canada" grew and grew. In the early 1700s, it even included lots of what's now in the United States. Later there was an Upper Canada, a Lower Canada, and a Province of Canada. Finally in 1867, when this country was officially formed, it was named...(c'mon, guess!)...CANADA!

Jacques Cartier

They could have called it Beaverland, instead.
Don't be silly, Bucko Beaver. Nobody would name a country after a beaver.
Why not? There's a country named after a turkey, isn't there?

Instead of a Kingdom, wouldn't it have been the Queendom of Canada, since Britain had a queen not a king at the time?

The Fathers of Confederation

The Kingdom of Canada

The Fathers of Confederation were the politicians who got together in Prince Edward Island in September, 1864, and started the ball rolling to create the country we now call Canada. They wanted to call it the Kingdom of Canada. But the British didn't think Canada should be a kingdom. So it became the Dominion of Canada instead. That idea of a dominion came from the Bible: "He shall have dominion also from sea to sea." From sea to sea—that sounded a lot like Canada! Today, we don't call it the Dominion of Canada. It's just plain old Canada.

Using the Name

Canadarm

The word Canada has been adapted to name other Canadian things. The Canadarm is the remote manipulator arm designed by Canadians and used on the space shuttles. With six rotating joints, it can grab satellites and other cargo.

The CANDU nuclear reactor was built by Canadians for generating nuclear power. CANDU stands for Canadian Deuterium-Uranium.

CANDU Reactor

I'm Canadian because... I can spell Saskachuwone. I mean, Sascatshoewun. No, I mean Saskatchewan. (Yeah, I did it!)

Saskachuwone
Sascatshoewun
Saskatchewan

That's me—cute, busy, and working hard to be your national symbol.

A Buck-Toothed Beaver Becomes a National Icon

What's short and squat, has a flat tail, buck teeth, and a big rump? Our national symbol, that's what. Okay, maybe a beaver is not as noble as the lion, Britain's symbol. Or as dignified as the United States' bald eagle. But Canada's beaver is, um...cute! And busy. Yes, beavers are very hard-working, chopping down trees to build lodges and dams.

Why Beavers?

How did beavers become a symbol of Canada? Back in the late 1600s, European gentlemen wore fancy beaver-skin hats. These hats were so popular in Europe that suppliers needed new sources of beaver. And guess what—across the ocean in Canada, there lived about six million busy beavers. To catch them, the fur traders needed help from the locals, the aboriginal people. So French and English traders arrived with trading goods such as blankets, guns, and copper pots. They traded these goods with the First Nations people for canoe-loads of beaver skins.

Are you serious? Canada got started because of some fashion trend in Europe?!?!

The fur trade took off! Fur traders made lots of money, and beavers became the symbol of Canada's importance to the world. What's more, while they were looking for furs, Europeans explored this vast and unknown land. Settlers arrived to start a new life here. The aboriginal people were outnumbered by the newcomers, and their way of life was changed forever. Over time, a railway was built from sea to sea. A new country, "Canada," was born. But it started with those beaver hats.

Beaver Operating Manual

Valves in the ears and nose close when underwater, like ear and nose plugs.

Special lids cover the eyes, like swimming goggles.

Flat tail makes a good paddle; also helpful for balance when standing on hind legs.

Outer hair is long and tough. The beaver's "underwear," the soft fur underneath, is what was used for hats.

Webs between the five toes of the hind feet, the better to swim with.

Mouth shuts behind the front teeth. That way, a beaver can hold sticks in its teeth as it swims, but keep water out of its mouth.

Chewing implements. The front teeth never stop growing! They get worn down with use.

Find the Beaver

Beaver fever! Flip a nickel and you'll see a beaver. Beavers also turn up on lots of other Canadian crests, stamps, and coins.

According to scientists, who like giving things Latin names, a beaver is actually a *Castor canadensis*. It's also Canada's largest rodent.

North West Company Beaver Token

"Three Penny Beaver" Postage Stamp from 1851

Hudson's Bay Company Coat of Arms

PRO PELLE CUTEM

A Goofy Beaver Souvenir

Canadian Pacific Railway Crest

Oops!

So many beavers were killed during the fur trade they were almost extinct by the middle of the 1800s. Fortunately, beaver hats went out of fashion in Europe. Instead, everybody went nuts over silk hats. Great fashion news, as far as the beaver was concerned. Today, the beaver has recovered and is alive, well, and very, very busy in Canada.

Treated Like Royalty

The moment the queen of England steps onto Canadian soil she becomes the queen of Canada. When you see her, you can bow or curtsey.

Queen Elizabeth II

Why Do We Have a Monarch?
Before Canada became a separate country in 1867, it was British. Even after Canada was formed, we kept our ties with Britain. Queen Victoria was queen of England when Canada was formed, so she became Canada's first queen. Today, her great-granddaughter, Elizabeth, is our queen. She doesn't actually run our country, though; we elect politicians to do that. The queen is the formal head of state for Canada. She officially represents the authority of Canada. That's why new Canadians pledge allegiance (duty and loyalty) to the queen, they are really pledging allegiance to the country of Canada.

Queen Victoria

The Queen's Representatives
The queen doesn't live in Canada so the government chooses someone to represent her—the governor general. The governor general lives in a huge mansion in Ottawa, Rideau Hall. It sounds like fun living there—there's a skating rink and toboggan slide in the yard. You always know when the governor general walks into a room—everybody stands up. And sometimes she gets a 21-gun salute, which would certainly catch my attention!

Queen Rachel

Rideau Hall

Nice try, Rachel. You have to be a member of the royal family to become queen.

Okay, I'll be the governor general, instead.

14

Happy Birthday, Queen Vic!

Canadians celebrate Victoria Day, the birthday of Queen Victoria, even though she died over a hundred years ago. Her birthday was May 24, so Victoria Day is celebrated on the Monday on or before May 24, to make it a long weekend. On that day, we also officially celebrate the birthday of the current king or queen of Canada, who happens to be Queen Elizabeth II at the moment.

The Great Seal of Canada

Really important government documents are stamped with the Great Seal of Canada. You put a document into the press, push down the handle, and it stamps an imprint on the paper. It's a picture of the monarch (Queen Victoria is shown here) in long robes, sitting on her throne, holding the orb (a round ball) and the sceptre (a staff—the symbol of royal authority). If a document has been stamped with The Great Seal of Canada, you know it's *Very Important*.

In England, the people celebrate Elizabeth's birthday in June, not May 24th. Is her actual birthday in June? No, it's April 21st. This is confusing—but just think of all the birthday cakes!

I'm also a great seal.

15

The Arms of Canada

Canada has arms, but not the kind you hug with. I'm referring to Canada's Coat of Arms. It's made up of pictures or symbols that together represent this country, and shows how we had two founding nations—France and Great Britain. Here's your guide to the Arms of Canada:

Don't confuse the Arms of Canada with Canadarm.

The Crest
The crowned gold lion, a symbol of valour and courage, has a maple leaf in its right paw.

The Imperial Crown
It shows that Canada is a monarchy—we have a queen (or king).

The Shield
Three royal lions representing England, Scotland's royal lion, Ireland's royal harp, and France's three royal fleurs-de-lis all appear on the upper part of the shield. Maple leaves at the bottom represent Canada.

The Supporters
The lion holds Britain's Union Jack flag while the unicorn holds French fleurs-de-lis on a banner.

The Ribbon
Desiderantes Meliorem Patriam is Latin for "they desire a better country." That's the motto of the Order of Canada, given to Canadians who have made a big difference to our country.

Canada's Motto
A Mari usque ad Mare is Latin for "from sea to sea."

Floral Emblems
Look for the Irish shamrock (three-leaved clover), the French fleur-de-lis (a white lily), the prickly Scottish thistle, and the English rose.

Latin is easy:

om-fray

ea-say

o-tay

ea-say.

That's pig-latin, not Latin! Ignore him, folks!

Ta-dah! Presenting...our version of a new Coat of Arms for Canada.
I'm glad that we replaced the lion, since there are no lions like
that in Canada. The goose is much better.
And I like the narwhal, that Arctic whale with a long, pointy horn.
It's much more Canadian.
Yes, I've never seen any unicorns in Canada.
And now we represent Canada's First Nations and
Inuit too—it's not all about the British and the French.

What a great new coat—it fits Canada very well!

WE SHOOT   WE SCORE

I'm sincerely glad it's not a coat made of beaver skins.

A Brisk Walk Around Ottawa, the Nation's Capital

Put on your sneakers, we're going for a walk around Ottawa. It's the official capital of Canada, so there are lots of very Canadian things to see.

We'll start our walk along Confederation Boulevard. It runs through Ottawa past the Parliament Buildings. The curbs and cobblestones are made of red speckled granite brought in from the Canadian Shield (the ancient, rocky landscape that surrounds Hudson Bay).

Next stop: The Tomb of the Unknown Soldier. Thousands of soldiers who've died in battle for Canada were never identified and lie in unmarked graves. One of these unknown soldiers now represents them all. His body was brought back to Canada from a grave in France, and buried here.

Here's the National War Memorial, honouring soldiers who died in World War I. This is where people gather at the 11th hour of the 11th day of the 11th month (in other words, on Remembrance Day) to remember all of Canada's fallen soldiers. The memorial shows soldiers moving through the archway from War to Peace.

Here are the Parliament Buildings—we'll check them out in more detail on page 21.

The National Aboriginal Veteran's Monument honours aboriginal Canadians who served in wars and peacekeeping operations. Can you see traditional Native symbols such as an eagle, bear, and wolf?

Watch out for lions! They prowl around Ottawa's buildings, keeping an eye on you. Lions are a symbol of British royalty so Canada, once a British colony, has a healthy population of big cats.

This statue stands on the lawn beside the Parliament Buildings. The headline on the newspaper the woman is holding reads "Women Are Persons!" The five women are celebrating the moment in 1929 when they won their legal fight to have the word "persons" mean both men and women. It's hard to believe, but before that, some people thought "persons" meant men only. Anyway, from then on, women could become senators and members of parliament—even be appointed governor general. Before that, they couldn't. Lucky they won that legal challenge. If women weren't "persons" with equal rights, how would I be able to become prime minister?

You're going to be prime minister? We need another legal challenge!

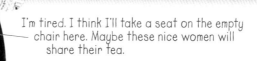

I'm tired. I think I'll take a seat on the empty chair here. Maybe these nice women will share their tea.

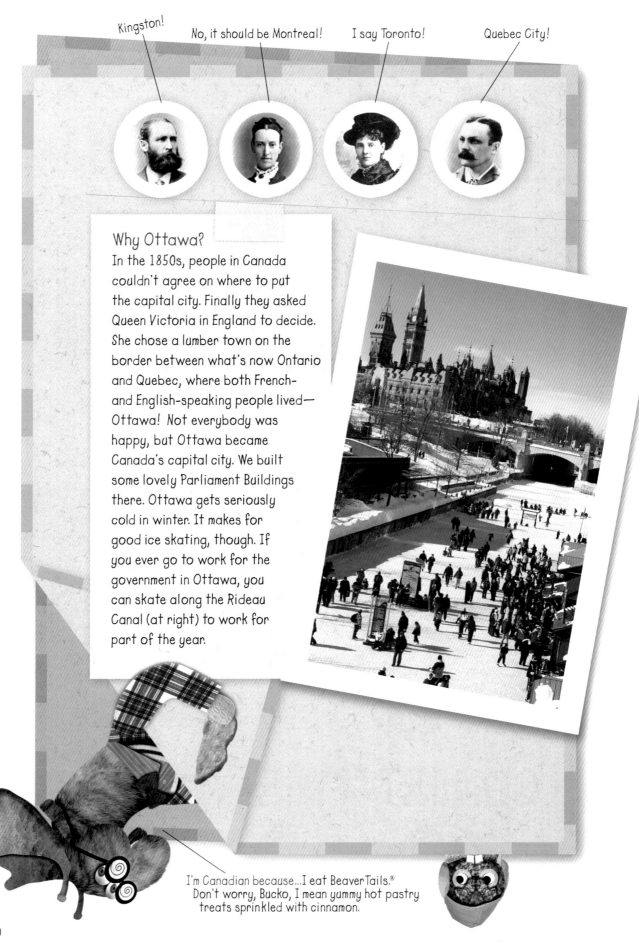

Kingston!

No, it should be Montreal!

I say Toronto!

Quebec City!

Why Ottawa?

In the 1850s, people in Canada couldn't agree on where to put the capital city. Finally they asked Queen Victoria in England to decide. She chose a lumber town on the border between what's now Ontario and Quebec, where both French- and English-speaking people lived—Ottawa! Not everybody was happy, but Ottawa became Canada's capital city. We built some lovely Parliament Buildings there. Ottawa gets seriously cold in winter. It makes for good ice skating, though. If you ever go to work for the government in Ottawa, you can skate along the Rideau Canal (at right) to work for part of the year.

I'm Canadian because...I eat BeaverTails.® Don't worry, Bucko, I mean yummy hot pastry treats sprinkled with cinnamon.

Are there any moose here?

Here's a tip: if you want to see Canadian symbols, you should visit the Parliament Buildings in Ottawa. You've never seen so many flags, coats of arms, provincial crests, and beavers! Don't worry if you can't make the trip. I did, and I'll fill you in. Step right up for my guided tour.

A Guided Tour of the Canadian Parliament Buildings

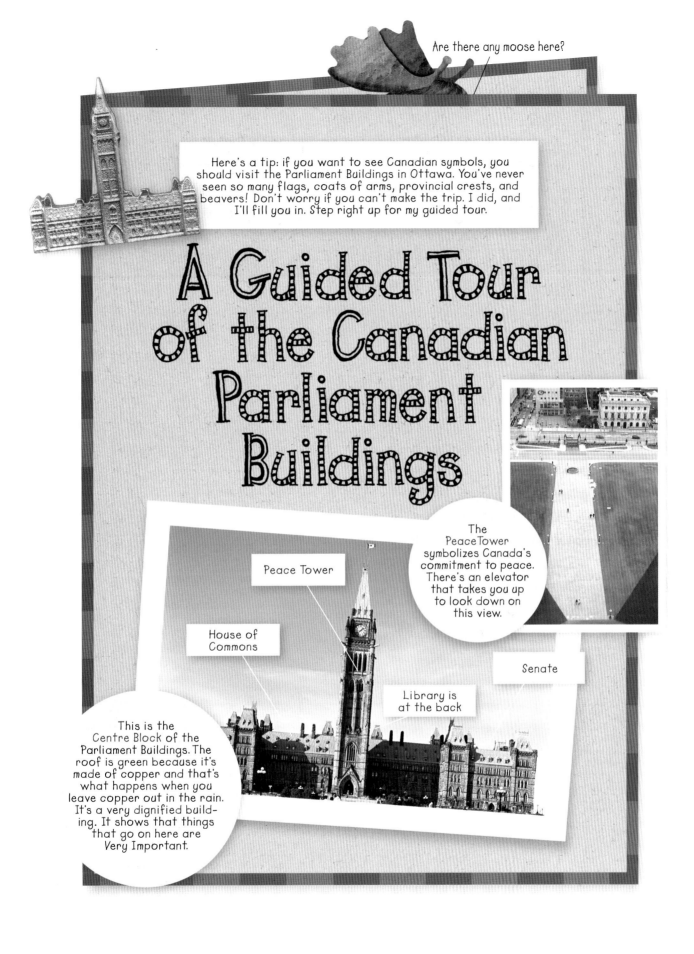

The Peace Tower symbolizes Canada's commitment to peace. There's an elevator that takes you up to look down on this view.

Peace Tower

House of Commons

Senate

Library is at the back

This is the Centre Block of the Parliament Buildings. The roof is green because it's made of copper and that's what happens when you leave copper out in the rain. It's a very dignified building. It shows that things that go on here are Very Important.

The Centennial Flame, in front of the Parliament Buildings, was built during Canada's Centennial (100th birthday) in 1967. It burns natural gas from Alberta. Around the border are symbols of the shields and floral emblems for all the provinces and territories that existed in 1967.

Meet a grotesque. He's a fantastical, mythical beast sculpted into the walls. Don't look now, but there are grotesques watching you everywhere in the Parliament Buildings.

How many of these provincial and territorial shields can you identify? (See answers below.)

Whose floral emblem is this? (See answer below.)

The floral emblem is the mayflower from Nova Scotia.

Provincial and Territorial shields: 1. Manitoba 2. Quebec 3. Saskatchewan 4. Ontario 5. Northwest Territories 6. Alberta 7. Prince Edward Island 8. British Columbia 9. Newfoundland & Labrador 10. New Brunswick 11. Yukon 12. Nova Scotia

Do you notice that Nunavut's symbol isn't around the Centennial Flame? That's because that territory didn't exist until 1999.

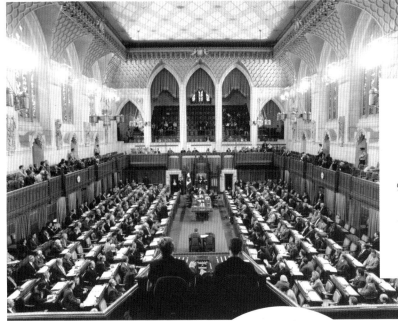

The House of Commons is where our elected Members of Parliament (MPs) meet to debate and make laws. It's more like a huge room than a "house." Its multitudinous (that means too many to be counted!) symbols include stained glass windows showing the flowers of the provinces and territories. And in the foyer, the hallway just outside, Canada's history is carved into the stone walls. You'll find explorers, voyageurs, gold panners, railway builders—it's all there!

Quiet in the Senate! The senators are discussing Very Important Business, like new Canadian laws. The Senate Chamber is all red and gold, with chandeliers and carvings and paintings of provincial symbols. It looks fit for a queen, which is handy because this is where the queen or her representative, the governor general, comes to make speeches to Parliament.

The Library: Winner, Most Canadian Symbols per Square Metre

I thought the Senators were an NHL hockey team.

The most incredibly decorated, symbolically loaded part of the Parliament Buildings is the Library. It's the only part that was saved when an earlier building burned in a fire in 1916. It has wooden walls and three storeys of wooden bookstacks, and they are carved with a gazillion flowers, coats of arms, masks, and mythical creatures.

It's official: I'm overdosed on Canadian symbols.

What's wrong? I was feeling very at home here.

I'm shocked that nobody suggested putting a stylish moose on the flag!

Much Ado About the Canadian Flag

Hoist the flag! The Canadian flag is the most recognized symbol of Canada. Red maple leaves flutter from flagpoles all across the country. It's even found in space—on Canadarm, the mechanical arm used on the space shuttles. But deciding on this flag was not an easy process.

The Flag Debate

Before 1965, Canada was using a flag called the Red Ensign. Note the Union Jack and the shield from the Canadian Coat of Arms.

The Red Ensign

The Canadian government started looking at ideas for a new flag in 1925. And again in 1946. Then again in 1964. Hey, no rush. In 1964, the government set up a committee to decide on a new flag. It received over two thousand ideas.

What about a Canada goose, flapping in the breeze?

Or a cuddly beaver?

Some of the flag proposals. Which is your favourite?

Red and white were already Canada's official colours. And for years, Canadians had been using a maple leaf as a national emblem. So many people thought the flag should include red, white, and maple leaves (as in the Coat of Arms). Some people wanted three maple leaves. Others formed "The Committee For a Single Maple Leaf" to push for just one. Prime Minister Lester Pearson wanted a totally Canadian flag, without any British or French symbols.

Prime Minister Lester Pearson

This was the flag Prime Minister Pearson liked.

The opposition wanted to keep a Red Ensign to show that Canada was still part of the British Empire. There was a furious debate in Parliament. It went on and on. When the prime minister finally ended the debate, his side stood up and sang "O Canada." The other side sang "God Save the Queen." Obviously, they still didn't agree. But majority rules, so we finally got a new Canadian flag. It looked like this:

The winner!

When You Make a Canada Flag
The flag is supposed to be twice as long as it is wide. The white part in the middle is an exact square. The red maple leaf has 11 points (no reason why—the designer just thought it just looked good that way).

I prefer lettuce leaves to maple leaves.

Rachel: did you know that people who study flags are called vexillologists?

But I bet they're not as vexing as you are!

Does it come with an operating manual?

How Does Canada Work?

Here's where I, Rachel, your loyal sleuth, help you figure out some things about Canada that I know have been really puzzling you. For instance, what is the Canadian Constitution? I bet you've been lying awake at night thinking about that one. You need wonder no more—I've figured it all out for you.

La Reyne le veult

ANNO TRICESIMO

VICTORIÆ REGINÆ.

CAP. III.
An Act for the Union of *Canada*, *Nova Scotia*, and *New Brunswick*, and the Government thereof; and for Purposes connected therewith.

WHEREAS the Provinces of *Canada*, *Nova Scotia*, and *New Brunswick* have expressed their Desire to be federally united into One Dominion under the Crown of the United Kingdom of *Great Britain* and *Ireland*, with a Constitution similar in Principle to that of the United Kingdom:

And whereas such a Union would conduce to the Welfare of the Provinces and promote the Interests of the *British Empire*:

And whereas on the Establishment of the Union by Authority of Parliament it is expedient, not only that the Constitution of the Legislative Authority in the Dominion be provided for, but also that the Nature of the Executive Government therein be declared:

And whereas it is expedient that Provision be made for the eventual Admission into the Union of other Parts of *British North America*:

Be it therefore enacted and declared by the Queen's most Excellent Majesty, by and with the Advice and Consent of the Lords Spiritual and

The Canadian Constitution

Canadian Constitution

When you make up a new country, you need to come up with rules for running it. So when Canada was formed back in 1867, we made up a constitution. It's our rulebook. It lays out how we Canadians govern ourselves. For instance, it explains that Canada is a "federation" with a government for the whole country as well as separate governments for each province. We also have a queen. We use both English and French languages in our federal Parliament.

You can't do something in Canada if it's not "constitutional" (not allowed according to the rules in the Canadian Constitution). All new Canadian laws have to follow the rules in the constitution.

You can't stop me chopping down trees. It's not constitutional! I know my rights!

Tell it to the judge.

Equal rights!   It's only right!   Darned right!

Right on!

In 1982, a new part was added to the Constitution—the Canadian Charter of Rights and Freedoms. It says that all Canadians have equal protection under our laws. You can be male or female, old or young. It doesn't matter what religion you practice, if you have purple hair, if you're disabled, if you're First Nations, or if your family came from Germany, Ethiopia, or the moon—you still have the same rights.

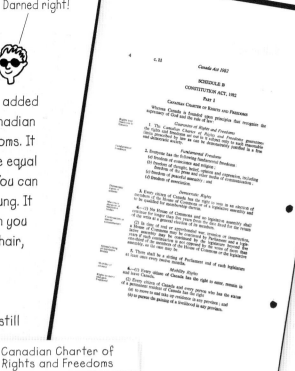

Canadian Charter of Rights and Freedoms

The Supreme Court of Canada

In this, the highest court in the land, the nine justices (judges) meet to rule on Canadian legal issues such as the Constitution and the Charter. The Supreme Court building is impressive. Statues of Truth and Justice guard the building. That's Truth on the left and Justice (in the cloak) on the right. After being carved in the 1920s, Truth and Justice were lost for fifty years. Someone found them in a packing crate under a parking lot. Finally they were put here, where they belong.

VERITAS

Truth

IVSTITIA

Justice

Yawn. Constitutions and Charters are boring. Like, who cares?

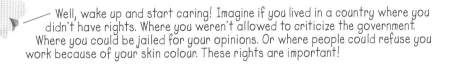

Well, wake up and start caring! Imagine if you lived in a country where you didn't have rights. Where you weren't allowed to criticize the government. Where you could be jailed for your opinions. Or where people could refuse you work because of your skin colour. These rights are important!

O Canada!

Recognize this tune? It's Canada's national anthem. Officially, it is supposed to be played "with dignity, not too slowly."

The very first version of "O Canada" was written in French and performed in 1880 in Quebec City. A musician named Calixa Lavallée wrote the melody. "O Canada" was officially made Canada's national anthem in 1980, a hundred years later. (Canadians don't make hasty decisions.)

These are now the official English words:

O Canada!
Our home and native land!
True patriot love in all thy sons command.

With glowing hearts we see thee rise,
The True North strong and free!

From far and wide,
O Canada, we stand on guard for thee.

God keep our land glorious and free!
O Canada, we stand on guard for thee.

O Canada, we stand on guard for thee.

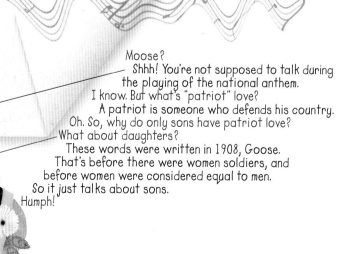

Moose?
Shhh! You're not supposed to talk during the playing of the national anthem.
I know. But what's "patriot" love?
A patriot is someone who defends his country.
Oh. So, why do only sons have patriot love?
What about daughters?
These words were written in 1908, Goose.
That's before there were women soldiers, and before women were considered equal to men.
So it just talks about sons.
Humph!

Here are two other English versions of "O Canada" written about a hundred years ago. Try singing them to the same tune.

[1]

O Canada! Our fathers' land of old
Thy brow is crown'd with leaves of red and gold.
Beneath the shade of the Holy Cross
Thy children own their birth
No stains thy glorious annals gloss
Since valour shield thy hearth.
Almighty God! On thee we call
Defend our rights, forfend this nation's thrall.
Defend our rights, forfend this nation's thrall.

[2]

O Canada, our heritage, our love
Thy worth we praise all other lands above.
From sea to sea throughout their length
From Pole to borderland,
At Britain's side, whate'er betide
Unflinchingly we'll stand
With hearts we sing, "God save the King",
Guide then one Empire wide, do we implore,
And prosper Canada from shore to shore.

Oops. Yogurt spill.

Stand tall, take off your helmet, and belt it out! "O Canada" can be sung before public events, at the start of each school day, when Canada gets an Olympic gold medal...or any time you feel an attack of Canadian pride coming on. It's okay to sing loudly and patriotically in the shower.

The women's hockey Team Canada proudly sing the national anthem.

Here's my version:
"O Canada! This sure is one great place.
From sea to sea, there's still a lot of space."

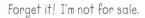

Forget it! I'm not for sale.

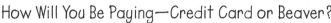

How Will You Be Paying—Credit Card or Beaver?

Money, money, money! Canadian money can take many forms. It can look like a $20 bill. It can look like a credit card. Or, as you'll see during our shopping trip back in time, money can even look like...a beaver pelt. Let's go shopping!

Shell Beads

Shell Beads

The aboriginal people living on the Pacific northwest coast did a great deal of trading with other First Nations. These long, white beads shaped like tiny elephant tusks were a highly valued trade item. They were made from *Dentalium*—small creatures found in the sea.

Coppers

Also on the northwest coast, a symbol of wealth among First Nations was a "copper." It was a shield-shaped plate of beaten copper that usually had a painted or engraved picture of an animal on its surface. If a chief could afford to own a big copper, it was a sign of his wealth and prestige.

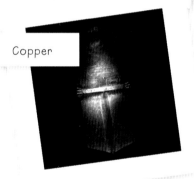

Copper

Wampum

In eastern Canada, First Nations people collected sea shells and drilled them to make cylindrical purple and white beads called wampum. The beads were threaded onto strings or woven into patterned belts. Wampum belts were like official documents; the bead patterns recorded treaties and other important events. When fur traders from Europe arrived on the Atlantic coast, they used wampum as a kind of money. The Europeans got wampum beads from the First Nations in return for guns, tools, and other goods. Then the traders took the wampum to tribes further inland and used it to buy furs.

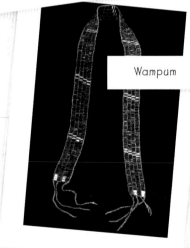

Wampum

So the IOUs were like cheques they could cash in later?

And in the meantime, they could play Go Fish with them.

Playing Cards

What, no money left? A bad situation for the governor of New France back in 1685. He needed to pay his military troops in Quebec, but it would be a long time before the next supply ship arrived with more money. So he took a deck of playing cards, wrote IOUs on the back, and gave them to the men.

Made Beaver

When First Nations trappers shopped for trade goods such as blankets, fire-arms, and copper kettles at trading forts in the northern wilderness, the cost of these items was shown in *Made Beaver*. A Made Beaver was one good-quality, adult beaver pelt. For example, a knife might be worth 1 MB (one Made Beaver), and a firearm 10 MB. Hudson's Bay blankets had the price woven right into the woollen cloth in short black bars. A blanket with four bars was worth 4 MB.

Money, Money Everywhere!

Banks were established in the 1800s, and each one issued its own bank notes. The notes promised that the bank would exchange the paper for gold or silver coins. Imagine how confusing that would have been with all those different banks issuing money! When Canada became a country, the new government got rid of all that old money and issued new Dominion of Canada notes.

Today's Paper Bills

Paper money today usually has the queen or a past prime minister on one side. On the other side is a picture of something else Canadian. On older bills, it's a picture of a bird. Newer bills show different things: children playing hockey outdoors; a picture called "Remembrance and Peacekeeping" and the poem "In Flanders Fields;" and artwork from famous Canadian sculptor Bill Reid.

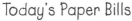

Check out the teeny, tiny printing on a modern Canadian bill. That microprinting makes money harder to fake.

I like this chocolate money myself.

Loonie Toonies and Piggy Banks ¢¢¢¢¢¢¢¢¢¢¢¢¢¢

Be proud: no other country in the whole wide world has a "loonie" for an official coin. We like our $1 loonie. We like it so much, we've now got a $2 "toonie." Who knows what we'll come up with next.

NEWSFLASH
Money doesn't grow on trees! The coins jingling in your piggy bank were made at the *Royal Canadian Mint* in Winnipeg, Manitoba, where they churn out 750 coins per second.

Do they also make those delicious chocolate-coated after-dinner mints?

No, Guy, making coins is a full-time job.

1¢ Pennies were once made of copper, but now they are made of steel with a thin copper coating. The copper is what makes them go brown. (And after a while, wet pennies go green.) Pennies have maple leaves on them.

5¢ Nickels are now made of steel coated with just a small amount of nickel. Maybe we should call them "steels" instead of nickels. Then we could say, "Don't steal my steel." Nickels show a beaver on a log.

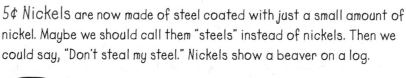

How about a 12-sided nickel? During World War II, brass was used to make the five-cent piece because all the nickel was needed for the war. To tell the brass coin apart from the bronze penny, they gave it 12 sides. That shape was kept even after the war when nickels were made from nickel again. Nickels returned to their round shape in 1963.

10¢ Dimes are also made of steel coated with nickel. They show the *Bluenose*, a famous Nova Scotian schooner (sailing ship) that won many races against American rivals in the 1920s and 30s. (Read all about it in the *Nova Scotia* section, page 52.)

Hey, how come I only get a measly nickel, but the loon gets to be on the dollar coin and the polar bear is worth two dollars?

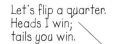

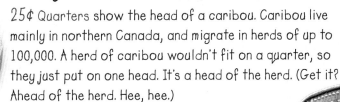

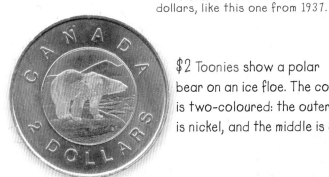

25¢ Quarters show the head of a caribou. Caribou live mainly in northern Canada, and migrate in herds of up to 100,000. A herd of caribou wouldn't fit on a quarter, so they just put on one head. It's a head of the herd. (Get it? Ahead of the herd. Hee, hee.)

$1 Loonies have a picture of a loon on them. The coin's bronze coating (bronze is mostly copper) gives it that gold colour. Real loons live in lakes and wetland areas. They have a haunting call, so when you hear a loon call at night, you are supposed to get Canadian shivers up your spine.

Long before loonies came on the scene there were silver dollars, like this one from 1937.

$2 Toonies show a polar bear on an ice floe. The coin is two-coloured: the outer ring is nickel, and the middle is aluminium bronze.

Flip a Coin

Queen Elizabeth II is on the back of our coins. (If you find one with King George on the back, it's really old.) Every now and then, the Mint has to come up with a new picture of the queen because she keeps getting older. She was 27 years old in the first picture, 39 in the second, 64 in the third, and 77 in the latest version.

I'm Canadian because... I carry loonies in my pocket.

33

Here's our task, Goose: we're going to brand Canada.

Brand Canada?

That's what they call it in the marketing biz. Branding Canada means coming up with a nifty little phrase or logo that we can use to advertise who we are.

So we need to sum up what Canada is all about in just a few words, Moose?

Right. We need a catchy slogan.

Okay, here's one: "Land of Honking Great Geese!"

Well, certainly wildlife is part of the Canadian appeal. I'll write it down. What about something with beavers, Canada's national symbol?

How about: "A Tail-Thwapping Destination!"

Or "A Country You Can Really Chew On!"

On second thought, maybe not beavers. What other animal is associated with Canada?

I know, "Canada: A Million Mosquitoes Greet You!"

That's welcoming, but it might make people itchy. Let's switch gears. Maybe something about Canada's natural wonders.

Like: "Discover Our True Nature."

Say, that's good, Moose!

But I didn't make it up. It's used by Canada's tourist industry. We need to come up with something else that captures the idea of our vast wilderness and wide-open spaces.

I've got it, "Canada: We've Got Lots of It!"

Catchy. But what is the "it" that we have lots of?

Bog. We have a lot of bog in Canada. Marsh and muskeg.

I can't see bog being a selling point for most people.

Then how about this: "Canada—Not All Bog!"

Hmmmm. Let's take a break and come back to this. It might take us a few sessions to come up with the perfect Canada brand.

Symbols from Sea to Sea to Sea

CHAPTER 2

Oops. Attack on Canada by the marauding dwarf rabbit.

Okay, fasten your seat belts because we're going on a cross-country trip. Each province and territory in Canada has its own symbols and emblems. From coast to coast (we'll go north to the Arctic coast, too), we'll find flags, coats of arms, maces, mottos, anthems, official birds, flowers, and more. Each province or territory chooses symbols that say something about that place—about the landscape, the people, the history, even the insects!

Every province or territory has an official coat of arms, just as Canada itself does (see page 16). Coats of arms usually have four parts: a Shield; a Crest on top of the shield; Supporters on either side, holding up the shield; and a Motto.

Crest

Shield

Supporters

Motto

You can put all kinds of symbols onto your coat of arms. Each symbol means something. Since much of Canada used to be British, we have some British symbols on our coats of arms, like lions, unicorns and flags. You'll also see French symbols, especially the white lily known as the fleur-de-lis.

If I made a coat of arms to represent my own family, the symbols would include our dwarf rabbit, a flower for my mom's garden, my dad's amazing cheesecake, and smelly socks to represent Guy's incredibly messy room.

Yes—a smelly sock! The official emblem of the Royal Society of Very Messy Rooms (RSVMR).

Hey—the sun is setting. Aren't you supposed to take down the flag at sunset?

Not again! Every time I put up the B.C. flag, somebody tells me the sun is setting and I have to take it down again.

BRITISH COLUMBIA

Rachel, B.C. is not just another pretty place!

Yeah, I know. It has slugs!

Do you think British Columbia is beautiful? The people who decide what goes on the licence plates certainly think so—the plates there say "Beautiful British Columbia." Think of snow-capped mountains and waves crashing on ocean shores. According to the tourist posters, it's "SuperNatural British Columbia!"

Why the Name?

British Columbia used to be...British. (Surprise!) It was a British colony, meaning it belonged to Britain even though it was here in North America. Actually, at first there were two British colonies: one called Vancouver Island and one on the mainland called British Columbia. They combined to become one, and that colony joined the rest of Canada in 1871.

What about the "Columbia" part? People started to call the area that's now the southern part of the province "Columbia" because the Columbia River flows through it. But there was another "Colombia" (with an "o") in South America. So this one in North America became British Columbia.

Beautiful British Columbia
ABC 000

British Columbia's Coat of Arms

Can you find:
• the Union Jack (because B.C. used to be a British colony)
• a setting sun and wavy blue and silver bars to show that B.C. is on the Pacific Ocean (where the sun sets)
• a wapiti (also known as an elk) and a bighorn sheep
• a royal lion (British symbol)
• a collar of dogwood flowers (B.C.'s official flower)
• motto: *Splendor sine occasu* is Latin for "Splendour without diminishment"

SPLENDOR SINE OCCASU

38

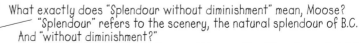

What exactly does "Splendour without diminishment" mean, Moose? "Splendour" refers to the scenery, the natural splendour of B.C. And "without diminishment?"

"Diminish" means to make something smaller. There's no diminishing B.C.'s splendour. Think of those huge mountains. Downright splendiferous!

Steller's Jay

I won! I won! I'm B.C.'s official bird. I beat the varied thrush, the rufous hummingbird, the harlequin duck, and all sorts of other bird-brains. The judges said I was inquisitive, smart, lively, mischievous, and noisy.

B.C. Ah, that must stand for **B**eautiful **C**ountryside.

Big **C**edars?

Buckets of **C**oastline?

Bear **C**ountry?

Bumpiest in **C**anada?

Banana **C**ustard

I'm a dogwood, a Pacific dogwood, to be precise—B.C.'s official flower. Woof, woof!

I'm a dog made of wood!

I'm a dog in the wood!

Pacific Dogwood

Banana Custard? Huh?

How's your Chinese?

卑詩省

That says "British Columbia" in Chinese. B.C. is sometimes called the "Gateway to the Pacific" because it's on the ocean and it's closest to countries such as China and Japan on the other side. Many immigrants from those countries have crossed the Pacific Ocean to live in British Columbia. The second most common language in British Columbia, after English, is Chinese.

ALBERTA

Okay, now oil tell you oil about Oilberta. Oops, sorry! I mean, I'll tell you all about Alberta. It's easy to get oil mixed up in Alberta because, after oil, there is a lot of oil there. But, wait, that's not oil there is in Alberta....

Very funny, Rach.

I know.
I'm such a gas!
(Get it? Gas?
Oil and gas?)

Why the Name?

Alberta was named for Queen Victoria's fourth daughter, Princess Louise Caroline Alberta. Lucky her name wasn't Priscilla or something.

Alberta's Coat of Arms

Can you find:
- the red St. George's cross. St. George is the patron saint of England, so his flag turns up fairly often. The red cross is also the official flag of the Hudson's Bay Company, the fur trading company that played a big part in Alberta's history.
- a scene with mountains, foothills, prairies, and wheat fields
- a beaver: the symbol of the fur trade that brought European explorers and settlers to Alberta
- a golden lion (for Britain) and pronghorn antelope (for Alberta)
- wild roses: Alberta's official prickle, I mean, flower
- motto: *Fortis et Liber*, which is Latin for "Strong and free"

NEWSFLASH

Alberta now has an official grass! (What will they think of next—an official vegetable?) It's a native grass called rough fescue. The province has the largest area of rough fescue in the world. (I'll bet you didn't know that. Do I get bonus marks, Mrs. G.?)

Fescue, eh?
A bit rough,
but it has a
pleasing,
grassy
bouquet.

I'm great, and horned! I can hear a mouse step on a twig 20 metres (65 feet) away, so don't try any funny stuff, mister. I'm watching you! (And I can turn my head 270 degrees.)

Great Horned Owl

Alberta's Official Flower: wild rose

Wild Rose

When Alberta schoolchildren chose an official bird, they chose the great horned owl, a fierce hunter and the largest owl on the continent.

Alberta's Official Toilet Tank Float

If you thought my homemade mace was silly, you'll think Alberta's first official mace from 1906 was hilarious. It was made in a rush when Alberta became a province and elected a government, but someone realized they didn't have a mace. Remember: a government can't start a session of Parliament and debate laws and stuff unless they first bring in the official mace (see page 9). So they made one quickly. It used plumbing pipe, a toilet tank float, old shaving mug handles, and bits of an old bedstead. By the time it was all painted gold, who would know? Alberta used that mace for 50 years!

Old Mace

The new mace has fancy decorations including a ring of precious stones. The stones are amethyst, lapis lazuli, beryl, emerald, ruby, topaz, and aquamarine. What word is spelled out by the first letters of those stones?

Rocky Mountain Bighorn Sheep

New Mace

It lives in the Rocky Mountains. It has big horns. It's a sheep. So guess what it's called!
A bull trout!
No, no, NO, Goose! Of course it's not a bull trout. It's a Rocky Mountain bighorn sheep—Alberta's official mammal.

I'm the bull trout, Alberta's o-fish-al fish.

41

Welcome to the Land of Living Skies!
Honk if you love Saskatchewan!

Honk! Honk! Honk!

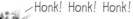

SASKATCHEWAN

Grab your broom if you're headed to Saskatchewan. Not because it needs a good sweeping. Because curling is its official sport!

Why the Name?

"Saskatchewan" comes from the Cree word *kisiskaciwan* meaning "swift-flowing water." It referred to the Saskatchewan River, which flows through the province.

Saskatchewan's Coat of Arms

Can you find:
- three gold wheat sheaves
- a beaver holding a western red lily
- a white-tailed deer
- Native beadwork collars
- maple leaf and western red lily badges
- Latin words *Multis e gentibus vires*, meaning "From many peoples' strength." Saskatchewan's motto refers to Saskatchewan's multicultural population, which includes aboriginal people and Métis (of mixed aboriginal and European heritage) as well as immigrants from many different countries.

Did I hear saskatoon-berry pie?

Saskatoon Berries

Berry good! If you love a piece of pie, then you definitely want to try saskatoon-berry pie from Saskatchewan. Purplish, almost black berries...sweet!

Saskatchewan's pretty flat, isn't it? They say you can see all of Saskatchewan by standing on a chair.

Ha, ha. Not true, Goose. The Cypress Hills in southern Saskatchewan are 1,392 metres (4,567 feet) high—the highest point between the Rocky Mountains and Labrador.

Okay, but there's often wind, right? They say you can always tell people from Saskatchewan because when the wind stops blowing, they fall over.

Very funny.

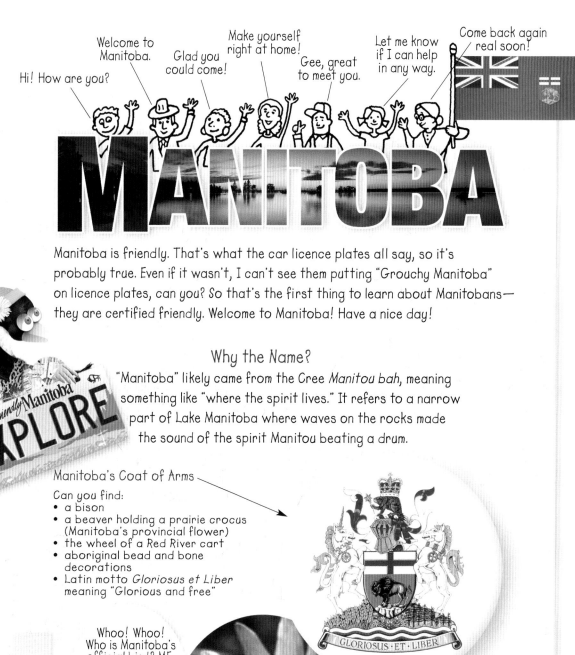

Hi! How are you?

Welcome to Manitoba.

Glad you could come!

Make yourself right at home!

Gee, great to meet you.

Let me know if I can help in any way.

Come back again real soon!

MANITOBA

Manitoba is friendly. That's what the car licence plates all say, so it's probably true. Even if it wasn't, I can't see them putting "Grouchy Manitoba" on licence plates, can you? So that's the first thing to learn about Manitobans— they are certified friendly. Welcome to Manitoba! Have a nice day!

Why the Name?

"Manitoba" likely came from the Cree *Manitou bah*, meaning something like "where the spirit lives." It refers to a narrow part of Lake Manitoba where waves on the rocks made the sound of the spirit Manitou beating a drum.

Friendly Manitoba
EXPLORE

Manitoba's Coat of Arms

Can you find:
- a bison
- a beaver holding a prairie crocus (Manitoba's provincial flower)
- the wheel of a Red River cart
- aboriginal bead and bone decorations
- Latin motto *Gloriosus et Liber* meaning "Glorious and free"

GLORIOSUS·ET·LIBER

Whoo! Whoo! Who is Manitoba's official bird? ME, that's who: the great grey owl. I'm North America's largest owl. From tip to tip, my wingspan is about 1.3 metres (4 feet 3 inches). Spread your arms out wide—about that far.

Great Grey Owl

Prairie Crocus

Manitoba's Official Flower: prairie crocus

Did you count them to be sure?

If you check Manitoba on a map, you'll see it has lakes a-plenty! Sometimes it's called "land of 100,000 lakes."

44

Caution: Buffalo crossing.

Bison Abound

Manitoba is also home to bison (sometimes called buffalo). Once, wild bison roamed the prairies in herds of thousands. Now they are almost all gone. There's a small herd in Riding Mountain National Park. But bison are still alive and well—as a Manitoba symbol. Look on the provincial flag, the coat of arms, in the provincial legislature where the government meets, on government signs, and even on Manitoba's telephone books. Everywhere you look in friendly Manitoba—friendly bison!

Red River carts are another Manitoba symbol. These handy two-wheeled carts carried loads across the prairies in the 1800s, over mud, marsh, and rivers. They were constructed of wood tied together with leather, and made an awful noise.

Polar Bears

Are a symbol of Manitoba's Hudson Bay area. Tourists flock to Churchill, Manitoba, in the fall to see them. Polar bears are Canada's largest land animals, and they are spectacular, but they are not friendly like other Manitobans. Do not shake hands with a polar bear. Did you know that a polar bear paw is bigger than a man's face?

I wonder who measured that polar bear's paw?

Look Up...Way up!

Up to the top of Manitoba's Legislative Building in Winnipeg. It's a bird, it's a plane...no, it's *Golden Boy!* He is actually covered with 23.4 karat gold, and weighs in at 1,650 kilograms (3,637 lbs) and is hard to reach. He holds a sheaf of grain in one arm and a torch held high with the other to inspire Manitobans to work hard for a prosperous future.

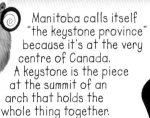

Manitoba calls itself "the keystone province" because it's at the very centre of Canada. A keystone is the piece at the summit of an arch that holds the whole thing together.

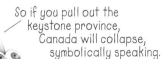

So if you pull out the keystone province, Canada will collapse, symbolically speaking.

45

ONTARIO

In Ontario, you can go jump in a lake. With over 25,000 lakes in Ontario, it's easy to do. Some, like Lake Ontario, are really "Great Lakes." And by the time you add up all this H$_2$O, Ontario has one-third of the world's fresh water. And if you don't want to fall into the water in Ontario, you can get the water to fall onto you—at Niagara Falls!

ONTARIO
AAAA ♛ 000
YOURS TO DISCOVER

Why the Name?
Even the name, Ontario, has to do with a lake. Historians agree that it's from an Iroquoian word—maybe *Kanadario*, *Onitariio*, or *Skandario*—that means "beautiful" or "big lake."

Rachel—
I guess if you're in Ontario, you should "lake it or lump it."

Ontario's Coat of Arms

Can you find:
• a moose and deer holding the shield
• a bear as the crest
• three golden leaves
• the Latin motto *Ut incepit Fidelis sic permanet*. It means "Loyal she began, loyal she remains."

VT INCEPIT   SIC PERMANET
FIDELIS

I'm the common loon. I'm Ontario's provincial bird. In a contest for kids aged 9 to 11, I was voted the most popular bird! I beat out the American robin, the ruby-throated hummingbird and the Canada goose.

Trillium

Ontario's Provincial Flower: trillium

Common Loon

You'll also find a trillium on all Government of Ontario signs. All in all, there are probably a trillion trilliums in Ontario, tra la!

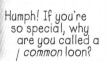

Humph! If you're so special, why are you called a *common* loon?

Dancing at the Caribana Festival, Toronto

From Far and Wide, O Canada

There are lots of people living in Ontario, about 12 million. That's way more than any other province. A third of all the people in Canada live in Ontario. Also, half of all the new immigrants (people from other countries) who come to Canada decide to live in Ontario, most in the capital city of Toronto. So if you want to travel the world—just go to Toronto! You'll find people from all different cultures and countries there.

While you're in Toronto, you could go up the tallest freestanding building in the world and look down—way down!—into Lake Ontario.

"Loyal she began, loyal she remains."

What's all this "loyal" stuff in Ontario's motto? I think it's to do with the United Empire Loyalists, Goose—the people who moved to Ontario from the United States because they were loyal to Britain.

Je me souviens.

QUÉBEC

Je me souviens. In English, that means, "I remember." It's Quebec's motto. What do people remember in Quebec? They remember Quebec's past, and how it was founded by the French. For years, it was called "New France." They remember that even though the British eventually took over Quebec, the people kept their French culture. French is still Quebec's official language. That's amazing, when you think about it. Quebec is surrounded by about 250 million English speakers in the rest of North America. TV and radio stations blast out English programs, yet Quebec is still mostly French-speaking.

Why the Name? (*Parlez-vous* Algonquin?)

According to the English, the province name is pronounced "kwa-bek." The French say "kay-bek." It's from the Algonquin word *quebecq* or *kebec* (it wasn't written down so there's no correct spelling) meaning "narrow passage" or "strait." It refers to the narrow part of the St. Lawrence River at Quebec City, the part that the English and French were always fighting over.

Quebec's Coat of Arms

Can you find:
- three fleurs-de-lis (white lilies, a French symbol)
- a blue-tongued, blue-clawed leopard (a British symbol)
- green maple leaves (they symbolize Canada, but Quebec is also known for its sugar maples)
- Quebec's motto (can you remember it?)

Quebec actually has an official provincial insect: the white admiral butterfly.

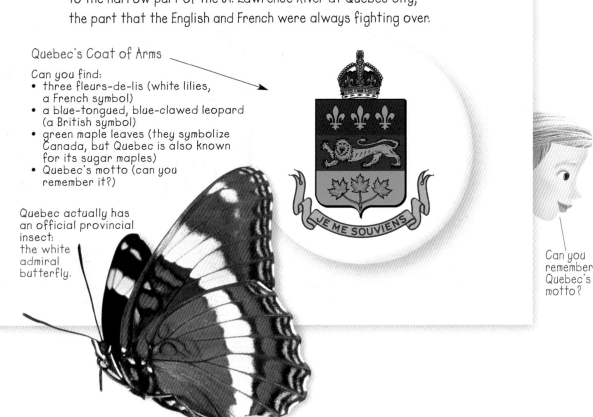

Can you remember Quebec's motto?

JE ME SOUVIENS

48

Salut! The yellow birch is Quebec's provincial tree.

Quebec's Official Bird: snowy owl

Snowy Owl

The fleur-de-lis (a lily flower) is a symbol of France that's now become a Quebec symbol. Way back in 1534, Jacques Cartier landed in Quebec and erected a cross that had fleurs-de-lis on it to claim the land for the King of France. Those symbolic flowers must have spread their seeds far and wide, because today you'll see fleurs-de-lis blooming on signs and flags all over Quebec. Four of them are on the Quebec flag, which is called the fleurdelisé.

Blue Flag

There was a big argument about what should be Quebec's official flower. The Madonna lily looked a lot like the symbolic fleur-de-lis. But it didn't grow naturally in Quebec. So since 1999, the official flower has been the blue flag, a kind of iris.

Winter!

Of all the seasons, winter seems to be a Quebec favourite. Many Quebecois play hockey or go skiing. They create ice sculptures; even build complete hotels out of ice. There's a Winter Carnival in Quebec City with a big snowman called Bonhomme. A famous Quebec song that starts, *"Mon pays, ce n'est pas un pays—c'est l'hiver!"* means (sort of) "My country isn't just a country, it's winter!"

Bonhomme, the Carnival's Mascot

I've forgotten Quebec's motto!
    I remember.
What is it?
    I remember.
What do you remember?
    Quebec's motto.
Good, because I don't. So, what is it?
    I remember.
Aaaaaaaaaah!

Yummy fiddleheads! Call the province "Fiddleheadland."

Or "Fundyland," because it's on the Bay of Fundy.

How about a name showing that both French Acadiens and English Loyalists settled here?

If you mix those words together you get... "Laocyaadliiesntss."

Catchy, isn't it?

NEW BRUNSWICK

Bonjour! Hi there! New Brunswick is Canada's only officially bilingual province—English and French are both official languages here. Yet the name of the province comes from Germany. (These things don't have to make sense.)

Why the Name?

New Nouveau Brunswick
000 000

The city of Brunswick, Germany, was once part of the Duchy of Brunswick (a duchy is land owned by a duke). When our Canadian New Brunswick was created in 1784, the Duchy of Brunswick belonged to the King of England. The King of England decided to call this new Canadian province New Brunswick, after the old Brunswick in Germany. People don't argue with the king.

New Brunswick's Coat of Arms

Can you find:
- Atlantic salmon wearing a crown
- two white-tailed deer with antlers
- friendship collars made of Maliseet wampum. (The Maliseet are one of the First Peoples of New Brunswick. Wampum is decorative beadwork made from shells.)
- shields representing Britain and France
- a British royal lion
- an old sailing ship
- purple violets (New Brunswick's official flower)
- fiddleheads (young ostrich ferns, still curled up, that New Brunswickers love to eat)
- the Latin motto *Spem Reduxit*, which means "Hope was restored"

SPEM REDUXIT

Why was "Hope restored" in New Brunswick?

The province's motto refers to the people called United Empire Loyalists, Americans who were loyal to Britain during the American Revolution. After the revolution, many United Empire Loyalists found a haven in New Brunswick, and so that's where their hope was restored.

Chickadee-dee-dee.

Black-Capped
Chickadee

New Brunswick's Official Bird:
black-capped chickadee

I'm a black-capped chickadee, New Brunswick's official bird. I think I should have been on the coat of arms. I'm a lot cuter than the fish.

New Brunswick's Official Flower: purple violet

Purple Violet

Ship Ahoy!

The ship that's on New Brunswick's flag and licence plate is the symbol that identifies the government of New Brunswick. That ship is an ancient galley, with oars and a sail. It represents New Brunswick's links to the sea. Shipping and shipbuilding have been historically very important in the province.

New Brunswick
Ship

I'm going undercover in New Brunswick. It's easy to do, since New Brunswick has more than 60 covered bridges. They're a New Brunswick specialty.

51

NOVA SCOTIA

Now would be a good time to start up a bagpipe tune. You see, bagpipes are Scottish, and Nova Scotia is exceedingly Scottish, too.

Why the Name?
Nova Scotia means "New Scotland" in Latin. See, I told you the province was very Scottish.

WATCH FOR PRICKLY THISTLES
(Thistles are very Scottish)

Nova Scotia's Coat of Arms

Can you find:
- two joined hands, one bare and one wearing armour
- a spray of laurel (a plant symbolizing peace) and a prickly Scottish thistle
- the blue cross of St. Andrew
- the royal lion of Scotland in the centre of the cross
- mayflowers (Nova Scotia's provincial flower) and thistles entwined
- a royal unicorn (another Scottish symbol)
- a 17th century artist's idea of an aboriginal hunter
- Nova Scotia's motto: *Munit Haec et Altera Vincit*, Latin for "One defends and the other conquers"

No doubt about it. You are a mayflower.

I *may* be Nova Scotia's official flower. I *may* be pale pink and I *may* flower in May. That's because I *may* be a *mayflower*.

Mayflower

Osprey

I'm an osprey, Nova Scotia's official bird. Smaller than an eagle, bigger than a hawk. I dive for fish and nab them in my talons.

NOVA SCOTIA
SAM 000
CANADA'S OCEAN PLAYGROUND

Welcome to Nova Scotia: Canada's ocean playground!

Blueberries

More Officialdom

Nova Scotia has an official dog, berry, and even a fossil.

Nova Scotia Duck Tolling Retriever

What's a Nova Scotia duck tolling retriever? No, it's not a duck. It's Nova Scotia's provincial dog. "Duck tolling" means luring a duck to within range of a hunter, which is what these dogs have been bred to do.

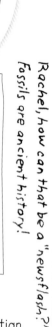
Rachel, how can that be a "newsflash"? Fossils are ancient history!

NEWSFLASH

Nova Scotia has a provincial fossil! It has a neat name, too: *Hylonomus lyelli*. Hylonomus looked like a cute little lizard. It is actually the oldest known reptile in the world. It was alive around 315 million years ago, way before the dinosaurs.

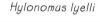
Hylonomus lyelli

Blue Noses

A *Bluenose* is not a nose; it's a ship. It's the famous Nova Scotian sailing ship that's on the Canadian dime. It was a fishing schooner (a real working ship) that won every race for 21 years against its American rivals in the 1920s and 30s. The original *Bluenose* is long gone, but Nova Scotians now have a replica—the *Bluenose II*. It sails up and down the coast to promote Nova Scotia tourism and trade. The *Bluenose* is an important symbol of Nova Scotian pride. Sometimes Nova Scotians even call themselves "Bluenosers." P.S. For your information, the *Bluenose* was not blue. It was black.

The *Bluenose II*

Hi there. Who are you?
I'm Prince Edward, Duke of Kent and father of Queen Victoria.
Hey—did you know that there's an island named after you?

PRINCE EDWARD ISLAND

Prince Edward Island may be Canada's smallest province, but it played a big role in the forming of the country. The so-called Fathers of Confederation gathered here in 1864 to come up with the idea to make the country of Canada.

Why the Name?

Prince Edward Island's been through a lot of names. The island's first residents, who were the Mi'kmaq, called it *Epekwitk*, meaning "resting on the waves." Europeans changed the pronunciation to *Abegweit*. Later, French explorers settled here and called it Île Saint-Jean. When Britain gained control, this was translated into St. John's Island. Finally, in 1799, the name Prince Edward Island was settled on, named after Prince Edward, Duke of Kent and father of Queen Victoria.

Blue Jay Feather

Prince Edward Island's Coat of Arms

Can you find:
- a sprig of red oak (the leaves turn dark red in the fall)
- a blue jay
- silver foxes: fur-farming of silver foxes was once an important P. E. I. industry. Foxes also apparently represent "sagacity, wit, and wisdom"
- a fishing net necklace, symbolizing the importance of fishing to P. E. I.
- a necklace made of potato blossoms, for P.E.I.'s biggest farm crop—spuds
- an English royal lion
- an eight-pointed star (a Mi'kmaq symbol representing the sun)
- flowers to represent P.E.I.'s founding nations: roses (England), white lilies (France), thistles (Scotland), and shamrocks (Ireland)
- lady's slippers, the provincial flower
- motto: *Parva sub ingenti*, which is Latin for "the small under the protection of the great"

P. E. I. is known for red soil. It's red from rusted iron.

Mrs G., I really had to dig to find this information. Bonus marks?

You can find me here any time of year. I live in the province all year round—I don't head south for the winter.

Blue Jay

P. E. I.'s Official Bird: blue jay

P. E. I.'s Official Flower: lady's slipper

Lady's Slipper

Hmmm. They don't look like they'll fit my feet.

ANNE of GREEN GABLES
BY L. M. MONTGOMERY

Red-haired Anne

When you visit P. E. I., you can drop in on Anne of Green Gables. (Note: she spells her name with an "e.") She's very popular. Thousands come to visit her home, which is pretty amazing since she doesn't really exist. She's just a made-up character in a story written by local author Lucy Maud Montgomery. Real or not, Anne has become a famous P. E. I. symbol.

"Prince Edward Isle, to thee
Our hearts shall faithful be
Where'er we dwell…"

This is part of P. E. I.'s "Island Hymn" written by Lucy Maud Montgomery, who also wrote the famous book *Anne of Green Gables*.

The highest point in the province is 152 metres (499 feet). Toronto's CN Tower is more than twice as tall.

Here's a skill-testing question for you. Labradorite is:

a) Someone from Labrador.

b) The owner of a Labrador dog.

c) The province's official gemstone.

And the answer is... c) The province's official gemstone.

NEWFOUNDLAND & LABRADOR

Watch out for the icebergs! Phew—just missed one. Icebergs are a spectacular symbol of Newfoundland and Labrador, but you don't want to run smack into them. Let's go ashore on "the Rock" and check out some other symbols.

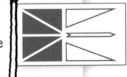

Newfoundland & Labrador
HJV 800

They should call it "Newfador." Or "Labraland!"

Why the Name?

Two names, actually: Newfoundland and Labrador, for the two parts of the province. "New Found Launde" was what King Henry VII of England called this land discovered by John Cabot in 1497. The land has been "found" for quite some time now, but the name has stuck. The "Labrador" part was officially added in 2001. The change was made to show that Labrador was an important part of the province, too.

Newfoundland & Labrador's Coat of Arms

Can you find:
- an elk. This makes no sense because there are no elk in Newfoundland, and never have been. Some people think maybe it was supposed to be a caribou (the province has lots of woodland caribou). The guy who did the drawing in the 1630s isn't around to sort out this goof.
- lions and unicorns—English and Scottish symbols
- Beothuk warriors with bows and arrows. The Beothuk were the original people living in this area, but they are now extinct. They all died or were killed.
- motto: *Quaerite prime regnum Dei*, which is Latin for "Seek ye first the Kingdom of God" and comes from the Bible

There is no sea life on the coat of arms! There's something fishy going on here.

My name is *Fratercula arctica*, but you can call me Atlantic puffin. Sometimes I'm also known as a sea parrot. Whatever you call me, I'm Newfoundland and Labrador's official bird.

Atlantic Puffin

Newfoundland Dog

Doggone! I'm a Newfoundland dog, an unofficial symbol of the province.

Not to be confused with me—the province's official *game* bird. I'm a partridge, or ptarmigan. I turn white in winter, which helps me blend into the arctic environment I usually call home. Some people call us arctic grouses.

Ptarmigan

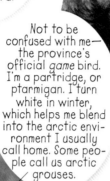

Pitcher Plant

The province's official flower is carnivorous. It lives in bogs and marshes. It gets nourishment from the insects that slide down its leaves and drown in water that collects at the bottom of the pitcher-shaped plant.

Raise the Flag!

There is no shortage of symbols on Newfoundland and Labrador's flag. Here's a rundown:
- white background to represent snow and ice
- blue for the sea
- gold arrow shows confidence, pointing towards the future

But also:
- the blue part of the flag near the pole that looks like the Union Jack, Britain's flag, is symbolic of the past
- the red and gold part points to the future (and also shows a three-pronged fishing spear, representing the province's ties to the sea)
- the outline of a maple leaf in the centre of the flag represents Canada
- the whole flag apparently looks like a Beothuk pendant. The Beothuk were the first peoples of this area, though there are none left today.

My pet rabbit is a big fan of Newfoundland and Labrador.

Anybody seen any gold?

Which way to the goldfields?
I hope I'm not too late.

To the Klondike! Join the gold rush! The famous Klondike gold rush of 1898 has become a well-used Yukon symbol. It's on all Yukon licence plates, for instance. But there's much more to the Yukon than a gold rush that happened more than a hundred years ago. Ready to check it out? Mush!

Why the Name?

Yukon is likely from the word *yukunah* in the Gwitch'i language or the Loucheux Indian word *Yuchoo*, both meaning "great river." That's the Yukon River they're talking about.

Yukon's Coat of Arms

Can you find:
- a malamute (husky) dog
- the cross of St. George, England's patron saint, representing early English explorers
- wavy up-and-down stripes in white and blue, symbolizing the Yukon River and the gold-bearing creeks
- gold circles representing mineral resources.
- Yukon mountains
- a blue and white pattern inside a circle to symbolize the fur trade: dark and light fur pieces were used to make designs like this

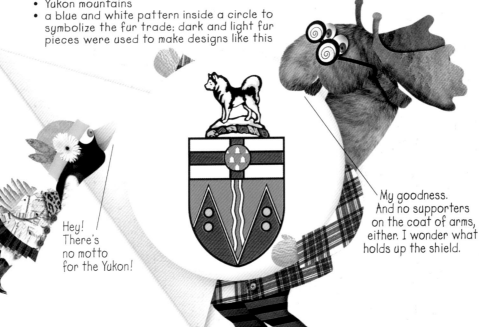

Hey! There's no motto for the Yukon!

My goodness. And no supporters on the coat of arms, either. I wonder what holds up the shield.

We'd better do something before it falls down!

This is a raven, the Yukon's official bird. It's like a crow but way bigger. You see them all over the Yukon—checking out garbage in Whitehorse or nesting in the cliffs along the mighty Yukon River. This bird is brainy, and an expert at snaffling food!

Raven

Fireweed

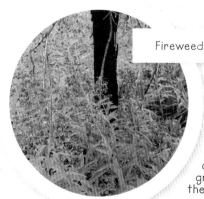

Yukon's official flower is the fireweed. Not only does it look beautiful when it blooms, but the young sprouts of fireweed are often cooked and eaten as greens. All parts of the plant are edible.

"There are strange things done in the midnight sun..."

So wrote poet Robert Service, a true Yukon icon. Actors now pretend to be Robert Service and recite his poems such as "The Shooting of Dan McGrew" and "The Cremation of Sam McGee." The tourists love it.

The Real Sam McGee

Woolly Mammoth

You'll see this fella with the tusks on signs and posters around the Yukon. It's a woolly mammoth, just one of the amazing, giant animals that roamed a land called Beringia, which includes northern Yukon, during the ice ages thousands of years ago.

Let's join the cancan girls! They came to the Yukon to entertain during the gold rush, and they haven't stopped dancing since!

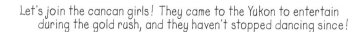

Gold! It's N.W.T.'s official mineral emblem.

All that glitters is not gold—we've also found diamonds. They're N.W.T.'s official gemstone.

Welcome to the Northwest Territories. Watch for animals crossing.

NORTHWEST TERRITORIES

Go north! Go west! (Oops—not too far west or you'll end up in the Yukon.) You're in the Northwest Territories. Keep an eye out for wildlife.

Why the Name?

It's the amazing shrinking Northwest Territories! Early Europeans called the whole north and west of Canada the North-west Territories. Then chunks were taken off to form the provinces of Manitoba, Saskatchewan, B.C., and Alberta, and also the Yukon territory. The part left over was still called the Northwest Territories. Then another big chunk was taken off in 1999 to form Nunavut. When that happened, some people in what was left of the Northwest Territories thought they needed a new name. In a name contest, somebody suggested "Bob," just as a joke, and it became the most popular choice! The government decided to stick with the old name.

Northwest Territories' Coat of Arms

Can you find:
- gold narwhals (a narwhal is a small whale with a protruding tooth)
- a compass "rose" (the diagram that shows north, south, and all the other compass directions)
- white to represent polar ice and wavy blue for the Northwest Passage, the sea route through the Arctic islands
- diagonal line across the shield symbolizing the tree line, green for the trees south of the tree line, and red for the tundra north of the tree line
- gold bars to represent minerals
- white fox to represent fur trapping

EXPLORE CANADA'S ARCTIC
000
NORTHWEST TERRITORIES

Polar bears catch rides on the back of N.W.T. vehicles.

Gyrfalcon

Mountain Avens

I'm a tough little mountain avens—N.W.T.'s official flower. Only the tough survive up here.

I'm a gyrfalcon, N.W.T.'s official bird. Excuse me while I hunt down this Arctic hare.

Arctic Hare

Hare today, gone tomorrow!

Northern Light Show

It's enlightening and illuminating: Northwest Territories is the place to see the huge natural fireworks known as the northern lights, or aurora borealis. Curtains of light shimmer, dance, and swirl across the sky.

I'm Canadian because... I know, from experience, that eyelashes freeze together at 40 below.

A coat of arms, or a coat of some kind, is definitely a good idea in Nunavut.

NUNAVUT

Welcome to Nunavut, Canada's newest territory. It's new, it's North, it's the land of the Inuit. And folks there didn't take long to come up with their very own symbols.

Why the Name?

Nunavut means "our land" in Inuktitut, the language of the Inuit. You can also write Inuktitut using syllabics—like the ones on the coat of arms. (By the way, "Inuit" means "the people" in Inuktitut.)

Nunavut's Coat of Arms

Can you find:
- an inuksuk: a stone monument that guides people across the land, or marks special places
- a qulliq: an Inuit stone lamp (it symbolizes light and the warmth of family and community)
- five gold circles representing the sun dipping below the horizon (in the Land of the Midnight Sun, the sun never sets in summer)
- north star: used for navigation across the snowy land
- iglu (igloo): a traditional Inuit dwelling
- tuktu (caribou) and qilalugaq, tugaalik (narwhal)
- three kinds of wildflowers
- the motto, in Inuktitut instead of Latin. *Nunavut Sanginivut* means "Nunavut our strength."

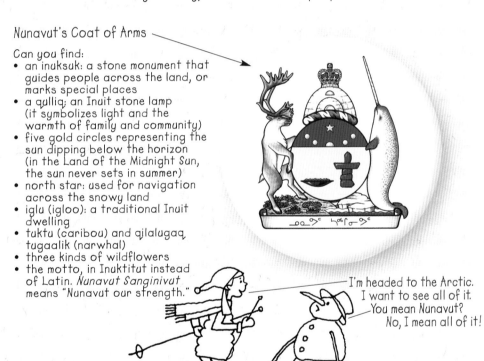

I'm headed to the Arctic. I want to see all of it.
You mean Nunavut?
No, I mean all of it!

Look familiar? After squabbling about it, both N.W.T. and Nunavut have decided to use polar bears on their licence plates.

EXPLORE CANADA'S ARCTIC
000
NUNAVUT

Rock Ptarmigan

Pssst.
I'm a rock ptarmigan
(don't pronounce the
"p"—say "tarmigan"),
Nunavut's official
bird.

Qummiq

I'm a qummiq, a
Canadian Inuit dog and
Nunavut's official animal.
I'm a hard-working sled-
dog, and perfectly suited
to survive in harsh Arctic
conditions.

Nunavut's Official Flower:
purple saxifrage (Did you
find it on the coat of arms?)

Purple
Saxifrage

North Pole

Quviasuktunga
tamaaniinnama means
"I'm happy to be here"
in Inuktitut. People in
Nunavut speak Inuktitut,
Inuinnaqtun (a form of
Inuktitut), English,
and French.

The North Pole is just a spot
on planet Earth. The Canadian
border extends that far but there's
no land there. It has become a symbolic
destination for polar adventurers.
Expeditions on skis, on dogsleds, or on
snowmobiles try to reach the North Pole
from Canada just to prove they can do it.
It's a challenge—an adventure!

But not polar bears. We just grunt.

WILL RETURN

Branding Canada:
EPISODE 2

I have a new idea, Goose. Let's think visually. Start thinking
of pictures or images that say something about Canada.
  To show that we're imaginative and creative, right?
  Indeed. By the way, the Canadian government already has a brand. It's called the
Canada wordmark and it consists of the word "Canada" with a maple leaf flag
over the last "a." Maybe we could do something along those lines?

I have an idea. How about this?
  What about some ideas that don't involve geese?
  Geese-less brands?
  Yes. I wondered if we could do something with
  a canoe? Canoes are very Canadian.

Like this? It shows that Canada is a wild,
  exciting ride! Wheeee! Go with the flow!
Hmmm. Looks a little dangerous, don't you think?

Or this! It shows that Canadians paddle
  upstream, persevering against the current,
  never giving up, never losing ground!
Well...

Or better yet, try this. This represents the multicultural
  nature of Canada—people of many cultural backgrounds,
  all in the same boat.
I wish the boat didn't look like it was about to sink.

I've got it! Try this one.
Why are they paddling in different directions?
  Because they're Canadian. They can't agree on where
  they're going. They're lost in the Canadian wilderness,
  probably seeking their Canadian identity.
I think you're getting a little cranky, Goose. Should we take
  another break? Then we'll give this branding exercise one more try.

Let Me Guess: You're Canadian!

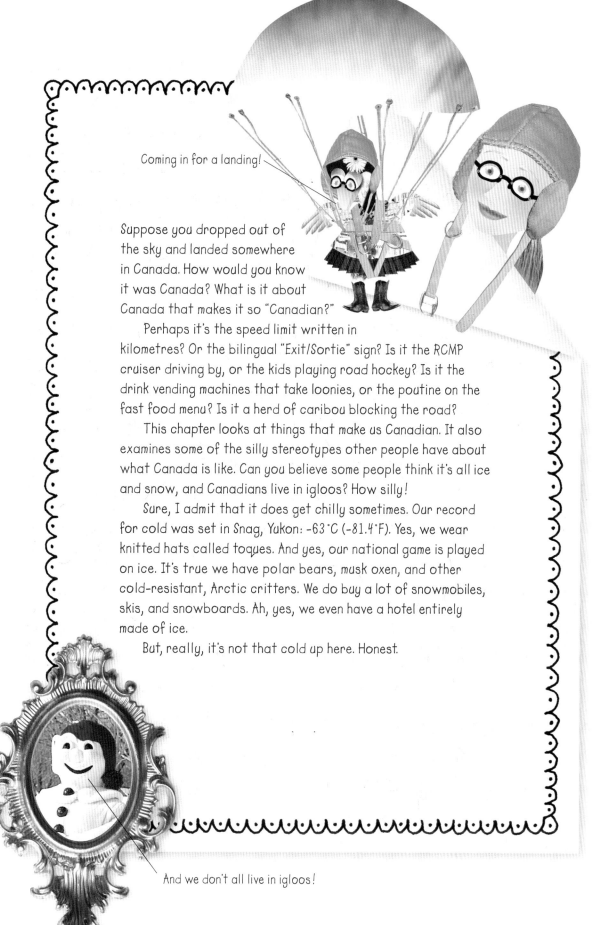

CHAPTER 3

Coming in for a landing!

Suppose you dropped out of the sky and landed somewhere in Canada. How would you know it was Canada? What is it about Canada that makes it so "Canadian?"

Perhaps it's the speed limit written in kilometres? Or the bilingual "Exit/Sortie" sign? Is it the RCMP cruiser driving by, or the kids playing road hockey? Is it the drink vending machines that take loonies, or the poutine on the fast food menu? Is it a herd of caribou blocking the road?

This chapter looks at things that make us Canadian. It also examines some of the silly stereotypes other people have about what Canada is like. Can you believe some people think it's all ice and snow, and Canadians live in igloos? How silly!

Sure, I admit that it does get chilly sometimes. Our record for cold was set in Snag, Yukon: -63°C (-81.4°F). Yes, we wear knitted hats called toques. And yes, our national game is played on ice. It's true we have polar bears, musk oxen, and other cold-resistant, Arctic critters. We do buy a lot of snowmobiles, skis, and snowboards. Ah, yes, we even have a hotel entirely made of ice.

But, really, it's not that cold up here. Honest.

And we don't all live in igloos!

Hey, hockey fans. Hockey's not the only national sport. Lacrosse is Canada's official summer sport, and it's been around longer than hockey. It was played by First Nations people here in Canada long before Europeans came along.

Hockey Night in Canada

It's a goal—the crowd goes wild! Wow! The excitement of a Saturday night hockey game. Hockey is a national sport, and a lot of otherwise normal Canadians are really crazy about this game. Who'd have thought that chasing a round piece of rubber across the ice with a stick would become such a source of Canadian pride.

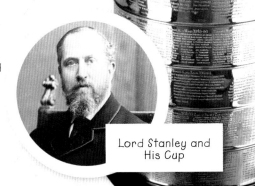

Lord Stanley and His Cup

Nice Cup, Stanley

Hockey historians argue about where the first real hockey game was played. Before that, kids just had fun with balls and sticks on frozen lakes. Probably the first organized game was in Montreal in 1875. Before long, teams started forming and challenged each other to games and tournaments. Canada's governor general in 1893 was Lord Stanley of Preston, and he had two sons on one of the teams. So he donated a trophy for the tournament winner—the Stanley Cup!

Luck of the Loonie

Canada was really celebrating when both the men's and women's hockey teams won gold at the 2002 Winter Olympics in Salt Lake City, Utah. Was it the lucky loonie? A Canadian worker putting down the ice at the rink placed a loonie under the surface at centre ice. The Canadian teams heard about the loonie, but kept it a secret until after the games. After both teams had won their medals, men's coach Wayne Gretzky and his assistant dug the loonie out of centre ice. It's now on display at the Hockey Hall of Fame in Toronto.

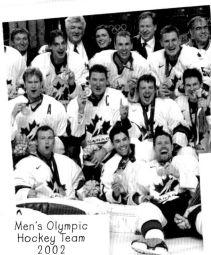

Men's Olympic Hockey Team 2002

Women's Olympic Hockey Team 2002

A Young
Wayne Gretzky

Hockey's the Game, Gretzky's the Name
Can you imagine trading away a Canadian hero?
That's what happened when NHL player Wayne
Gretzky, "the Great One," the highest scorer
of all time, was traded by the Edmonton Oilers
to the Los Angeles Kings in the United States.
It made front-page headlines across Canada.
How could this happen? Gretzky was our star
player, and he was a Canadian—born in
Brantford, Ontario. It was unthinkable!

A rabid hockey fan.
(Get it? Rabbit hockey fan!)

That Goal

Ask anyone over 40 about Paul Henderson's
famous goal. They'll know what you mean.
It was September 28, 1972. Team Canada
was playing its rival, the Soviet Union
(which back then included Russia and neighbouring countries).
It was Game eight—the deciding game. Canada and the Soviet Union were even
at three games each, plus a tie. Going into the third period, Canada was
down three goals to five. Then Team Canada scored two goals to
even the score. By now, even people who never watched hockey
games were glued to their TVs. Canadians were holding their
breath. And then, with just 34 seconds remaining in the
game, Paul Henderson shot the winning goal under
the Soviet goalie. "They score! Henderson
has scored for Canada!" yelled broad-
caster Foster Hewitt. From coast to coast,
millions of Canadians cheered, danced,
hugged, and went bonkers!

Wayne Gretzky was the
greatest hockey player
of all time!
No way, it was
Mario Lemieux.
Bobby Orr.
Gordie Howe had
incredible strength.
But what about Bobby
Hull's slapshot.
Phil Esposito was the man.
"Rocket" Richard scored
50 goals in a season.
So, you ever heard of Joe Malone?
He scored 44 goals in 20 games
back in 1917–1918!

69

I'm a Francophone on the saxophone.

I'm an Anglophone on the sousaphone.

Parlez-vous Canadian?

Hello?

Bonjour?

We have lots of phones in Canada. It can get rather noisy!

rue **Sparks** St.
240 → 440

My cereal box says, *"Le goût carrémont bon...."* The other side says, "Good, good whole wheat...." It's a clever, bilingual cereal box. It talks in both of Canada's official languages. We are the only country in the world to be officially bilingual. ("Bi" means two, and "lingual" means language). Not everybody speaks two languages, of course, and lots of Canadians speak other languages too, but the government of Canada uses both English and French.

Cherchez le français!

About one quarter of Canadians are Francophones. They speak French as their main language. Most Francophones live in Quebec, but there are French communities across Canada, especially in Ontario, New Brunswick, and Manitoba. In Atlantic Canada, the Francophones are descendants of the French-speaking Acadians who settled in the area back in the 1600s. New Brunswick is Canada's only officially bilingual province.

ARRÊT

Stop! On second thought, *Arrêt!* In Quebec all signs are in French, the province's official language. Elsewhere, signs are often bilingual.

Pick up and take away your animal's waste

Emportez les excréments de votre animal

$ **minimum** **100**

SALE VENTE 30 TO 50%

TOW AWAY ZONE

ZONE DE REMORQUAGE

Why is Canada Bilingual?

Canada is bilingual because it has two founding nations. (Of course, that's only true if you ignore the First Nations who were living in Canada at the time. Back then, they were frequently ignored.)

Explorer Jacques Cartier claimed it for France in 1534. But after the British arrived, there were centuries of squabbling over who would get Canada. The British and French shot muskets and cannons at each other, and didn't share nicely. Finally in 1753, not long after a famous battle on the Plains of Abraham near Quebec City, France handed Canada over to Britain. That meant it was British, even though most people living here spoke French. Later more English settlers arrived, including thousands of British United Empire Loyalists from the United States.

The languages are leaking! French words such as dépanneur (corner store) and Métro (subway) are ending up in English. Meanwhile, English words such as "bluejeans" and "weekend" creep into French.

I'll buy milk at the dépanneur on the way home from the Métro.

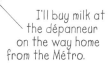

Le weekend je porte des jeans.

Rachel's Canadian Café

Welcome to Rachel's Canadian Café! Serving tasty treats from across the country—both traditional dishes from way back and current favourites. Today's special is yummy muktuk—whale skin lined with a thin layer of fat. It's an Inuit specialty with a tender-crisp texture and a taste like fresh coconut. Try dipping it in soy sauce.

APPETIZERS

Cod Lips and Cod Cheeks: The tastiest morsels of this fish that sparked the cod rush and lured thousands of fishermen from Europe to our Atlantic shores five hundred years ago. Limited supplies only!

Beaver Tail: Roasted over a campfire, skinned and sliced.

Jellied Moose Nose: Simmered in a broth and then cooled until it turns to jelly.

Salt Cod: Taste a piece of Canada's history that's still served up on the east coast today. Dried, lightly salted cod—as valuable as gold to the Europeans fishing off Newfoundland's shores hundreds of years ago.

Dulse: Purple seaweed, sun-dried on the rocks of New Brunswick. Indescribable!

SOUP OF THE DAY

French Canadian Pea: Simmering cauldron of yellow peas, salt pork, and onions.

QUICK MEALS

Pemmican: Made-in-Canada energy bar used by fur trade voyageurs on the go. Buffalo meat is pounded and then mushed up with fat and berries.

Poutine (pronounced "poo-teen"): A Quebec specialty that started when restaurant owner Fernand Lachance put french fries and cheese curds in the same bag for a customer who wanted both to take out. He called the gucky mess "poutine" and the combo was so delicious he added it to his menu. Later, people started adding gravy.

Bannock: This traditional bread was brought to Canada by Scottish fur traders and adapted to the campfire by First Nations cooks. We use traditional ingredients—flour, salt, bacon grease, and water—and fry the bread dough in a pan with butter. So yummy!

All meals come with french fries—Canada's favourite food. Canadians eat their weight in potatoes every year.

VEGETABLE SIDE DISHES

Steamed Fiddleheads with Garlic Sauce: We pick tender, tasty young ferns from New Brunswick before they uncurl and become big ferns.

Wild Rice: For thousands of years the Ojibwa people have harvested this grain (it's not really rice) from the marshes of Ontario and Manitoba. The long plant stalks are bent over a canoe and flailed with a paddle, which makes them drop their grains. These are dried then roasted nut-brown.

SEAFOOD SPECIALTIES

Atlantic Lobster: How can something that scary-looking taste that good?

Smoked Wild Pacific Salmon: A staple of the diet of the First Nations living along the Pacific coast, and now a gourmet treat shipped around the world.

Arctic Char: This northern fish has a legendary taste.

MEAT DISHES

Tourtière: Quebec's classic meat pie made with pork, potatoes, onions, and spices.

Beefalo Burgers: Gone are the days when herds of bison roamed the prairies, but you can get a taste of that bygone time with these meaty burgers, a cross between buffalo and beef.

Roast Canada Goose: We stuff our fowl with Canada's famous McIntosh apples. Today there are more than three million McIntosh trees in North America. They all started from the one tree that John McIntosh found on his farm near Prescott, Ontario, in 1811.

DESSERTS

Bakeapple Pie: Fresh from a Canadian bog, the berries, also called cloudberries, look like yellow raspberries and taste like tart peaches.

Saskatoon Berry Cheesecake: Ask anyone from Saskatchewan about the delicious taste of saskatoons.

Wild Blueberry Grunt: A Maritime favourite, fruit with a cake-like topping. You'll grunt with pleasure!

Nanaimo Bars: From Nanaimo, British Columbia. A graham cracker base and a layer of custard icing topped with melted chocolate. Oh my!

Skedaddle Cookies: from Skedaddle Ridge, New Brunswick.

Maple Syrup Fudge: Everyone loves the sweet taste of maple syrup. Did you know that Canada supplies more than three-quarters of the world's supply?

Boycott the roast goose! Try apple pie instead.

Rachel, I read that it takes about 150 litres (40 gallons) of sap from a maple sugar tree to make just four litres (one gallon) of maple syrup. That's a lot of sap!

Very sweet of you to pass that on!

73

Can you paddle a canoe?
It's a very Canadian thing to do!
Grab your paddle and I'll show you the strokes.

Different Strokes for Different Folks

Canada's First Nations people were our first paddlers. Their traditional Algonquian canoe design remained unchanged for thousands of years. A wood frame was covered with birch bark and glued with gum from spruce trees. Birch bark canoes were the ideal way to cover territory. They were pretty much the only way to get across shallow, marshy areas. They were easily steered around rocks, light enough to portage (carry) around waterfalls, and handily repaired en route with more birch bark and spruce gum.

Birch Bark Canoe

At first, European explorers who arrived in Canada weren't sure about canoes. They seemed kind of tippy. But canoes turned out to be the best way to explore the country. So the Europeans hired First Nations paddlers and guides who knew a thing or two about wilderness canoeing.

First Nations living on the Pacific coast made dugout canoes by hollowing out cedar trees. The Haida built ocean-going ones that were longer than a big moving van. Portaging not recommended.

Dugout Canoe

Canoe transport was replaced by trains, planes, and 18-wheeled transport trucks. Canoes are now used for recreation. On modern canoes, the birch bark covering has been replaced by canvas, aluminum, fibreglass, or a really tough, space-age plastic.

Quit splashing me!

Hey, bad news! I think I can hear a waterfall ahead.

Canoes were used by the voyageurs during the fur trade to transport supplies through the boggy, soggy, mosquito-infested wilderness to fur trading forts dotted throughout the northwest. On the return trip the canoes were loaded down with furs. Canots du nord were used on northern rivers. Canots de maître were big freight canoes used on the southern route.

The voyageurs paddled from dawn to dusk, 18 hours a day, for six weeks at a time. They raced through dangerous rapids, leapt out of the canoe into the rushing water to lift the boats off the rocks, and hauled loaded canoes upstream against the current. No couch potatoes, these voyageurs.

The canoe race across the Saint Lawrence River is still the most popular event at Quebec's winter carnival. Teams battle ice floes, slush, open water, river currents, and wind as they paddle, haul, and shove their canoes across the river. What can I say—it's a very Canadian thing to do! This grueling race, started in 1894, celebrates the bravery of those who used to deliver mail and supplies to Quebec City across the ice-clogged river in winter, back before bridges were built.

"Toque" is another Canadian word.

Has anyone seen my mittens? I can't remember where I left them.

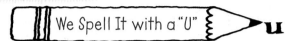

We Spell It with a "U"

When you were little, did you have idiot strings on your mittens to keep them attached to your coat? I did! You might know what idiot strings are, but people from other countries wouldn't have a clue. That's because "idiot strings" is a Canadian term, something we've made up and added to our language.

In Canada, we speak Canadian English. Sometimes it's like the English spoken in Britain. Sometimes it's more like the English spoken in America. And some words and spellings are our very own invention. Take this quiz to test your knowledge of spelling the Canadian way.

First question. How do you spell words such as colour, honour, and labour?

Without a "u" — Team U.S.A.

With a "u" — Team Britain

With a "u" — Team Canada

What are the last two letters in "centre" and "theatre"?

E-R — Team U.S.A.

R-E — Team Britain

R-E — Team Canada

Did you know that "muskeg" is a Canadian word for bog? I thought not. Now you know.

What do you call those four round rubber things that hold up a car?

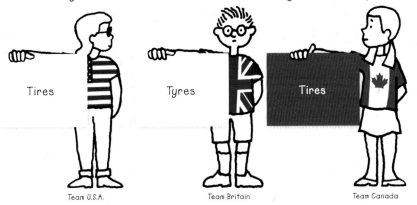

Tires
Team U.S.A.

Tyres
Team Britain

Tires
Team Canada

What colour is an elephant?

Gray
Team U.S.A.

Grey
Team Britain

Grey
Team Canada

What's the last letter in the alphabet?

Zee
Team U.S.A.

Zed

Zed
Team Britain

You're both ruining your teeth!

I'm Canadian, so I drink cans of pop.

I'm American, so I drink cans of soda.

Send in the Mounties

Throughout the world and on TV, the Royal Canadian Mounted Police (or Mounties for short) are recognized as a symbol of law, order—and Canada. They've been cast as heroes in hundreds of Hollywood movies. They're featured on posters and postcards. They're the good guys (and gals) in red coats and Stetson hats, riding to the rescue.

Rachel's Fast History of the Mounties

Trouble at Cypress Hills

It started in what's now southern Alberta. Whiskey traders and wolf hunters from the United States shot and killed a large party of Assiniboines they accused of stealing horses. There had been trouble before with whiskey traders selling bad drink to the Native people in return for furs. As for the wolf hunters, they were using poisoned buffalo bait to catch wolves, and it was also poisoning dogs from First Nations tribes. Things were getting out of hand in the west. Send in the Mounties!

No roads or railways or bridges!

I'm hungry and thirsty.

Why did I sign up for this?

I'm cold!

We're building character!

The Great March West

The newly created North-West Mounted Police rode westward in 1874. It was an epic, grueling trip of 1,500 kilometres (930 miles) over several months. When the Mounties finally reached the whiskey traders' base at Fort Whoop-Up in the foothills of the Rocky Mountains, the traders had fled. The Mounties went to work: they stamped out the illegal whiskey trade, kept the peace, and made treaties with First Nations of the Plains such as the Blackfoot. They kept order as waves of white settlers and railway builders moved onto the prairies.

CANA

Gold
Discovered!
From then on, the
NWMP were dispatched
whenever there was a need
for law and order. During
the Klondike Gold Rush,
the Mounties controlled
thousands of American
miners headed for
the Yukon.

RCMP Cruiser

NWMP Becomes the RCMP

In 1920, the North-West Mounted Police were renamed the Royal Canadian
Mounted Police. Today there are over 20,000 RCMP members enforcing the law
in every province and territory (except Ontario and Quebec, which have their
own provincial police forces).

RCMP Musical Ride

What Happened to the Horse?

The Mounties have dismounted. Actually, they
quit using horses for regular duties in the late
1930s. Regular recruits haven't learned to ride
since 1966. Almost the only place you'll see
mounted Mounties these days is in the RCMP
Musical Ride—a performance of cavalry
riding skills featuring hundreds of Mounties
on horseback.

Hey, where's
your red coat?

It looks sharp
but it's not
practical for
everyday work.
I only use the
red serge and
the Stetson hat
for formal
occasions.

79

Supersized Canada— It's Wild Out There!

Canada is the second biggest country in the world. Some people have an image of Canada as being all a vast wilderness. They see it as home to free-roaming wildlife like bears and moose, and the only people who live in Canada are Indians in canoes and lumberjacks in red plaid shirts.

Does that sound like downtown Toronto or Vancouver? Apparently the word hasn't gotten out that we have cities, suburbs, strip malls, and traffic jams here in Canada. But it's true that, once you head away from the cities, Canada can be a vast and awesome land.

Water, Water Everywhere!
- Canada has the longest coastline in the world.
- Canada has most of the world's fresh water.
- Lake Superior is the largest freshwater lake in the world.
- More water rushes over Niagara Falls than any other waterfall in the world.
- The largest wetland in the world is around Hudson Bay. (Did you bring a towel?)

Are you feeling waterlogged yet?

Helloooooooooo

Where Is Everybody?
Canada has lots of empty space, especially up north. Most Canadians live in the south, along the United States border. If you were to spread Canadians evenly over the whole country, there would be about 3.2 people per square kilometre (half-mile squared). (I'm not sure what the .2 person would look like.)

Canadian Wildlife Sightings

A symbol of Canada's Arctic, the polar bear is the biggest bear there is, weighing as much as a small car. It gobbles ringed seals for breakfast. It can sniff out their breathing holes a kilometre (0.6 miles) away, even covered by ice and snow. Little bumps and hollows on its feet act like suction cups so it doesn't slip on the ice.

Grizzly Bears are a perfect symbol of Canada's wilderness, because they can't stand to have people around. A grizzly bear is a solitary guy and needs its personal space. It can't survive without wilderness.

Caribou herds crossing the tundra is a very Canadian image. Not that most Canadians ever see caribou, since they roam the North. They are incredible navigators, travelling hundreds of kilometres each spring to end up back at the calving area they left the year before.

Moose are shy and solitary. You'll be lucky to spot one. The moose might not spot you, either—it has terrible eyesight! But it will hear and smell you. Moose have no problems with Canada's cold winters. If it's a hot, buggy summer, you'll find them chillin' in the pond.

Go away.

Bugs—mosquitoes, blackflies, and horse-flies especially—are also identified with Canada. Horseflies have been described as teeth with wings. Mosquitoes zero in on your blood with chemical sensors to detect your breath and sweat. Visual sensors that lock on anything that moves (if it moves, it's probably full of blood), and heat sensors that detect a warm body. You're doomed!

Dwarf rabbit sighting.

Whoa!

81

Meet the Neighbours

Okay, imagine this scenario. There's this little mouse that lives beside an elephant. It's tricky for the mouse, because it could accidentally get squished by the elephant. The elephant is friendly, but it might roll over without even noticing the mouse is there.

What am I talking about? I'm talking about Canada and the United States. Canada has only about 32 million people, but America has nine times that. So we're like a mouse living beside an elephant. We could be overshadowed by our neighbour, or overlooked, or even crushed. In fact, during the War of 1812, we almost were. But instead, Canada has remained a separate and independent country.

American Thanksgiving is in late November.

By then it's winter in Canada. So Canadians celebrate Thanksgiving earlier, on the second Monday in October.

I'll be sure to mark that on my calendar.

How do you make sure the elephant knows you're there?

I squeak. And if that doesn't work, I nibble its toes!

We have something the Americans don't have—a queen.

Canada is made up of ten provinces and three territories. America, on the other hand, is made up of states—50 of them.

American paper money has always been green (that's how the bills got the name "greenbacks"), though bills are now being made with subtle colouring. Canadian paper bills, on the other hand, come in a rainbow of different colours. Another difference: an American dollar is worth more than a Canadian one.

Both Canadians and Americans celebrate Christmas and New Year's, but other holidays are different. Only Canadians celebrate Victoria Day. Only Americans celebrate President's Day and Martin Luther King Day. Canadians set off fireworks on Canada Day, July 1st. Americans have their party on Independence Day, three days later.

Canadians use metric measurements—kilometres instead of miles. (Since kilometres are shorter, Canadians have to drive more of them to get where they're going.) Canadians drive on "highways" while Americans drive on "freeways."

Canada's top dog is the prime minister. America's head honcho is the president.

In Canada, the first book in the Harry Potter series was called *Harry Potter and the Philosopher's Stone*. The publisher didn't think that title would appeal to American readers, so the U. S. version was re-named *Harry Potter and the Sorcerer's Stone*.

In Canada, I freeze at 0° Celsius.

Well, I freeze at 32° Fahrenheit in the United States.

What do you say we all go in for hot chocolate?

83

EH!

Hop onto Rachel's Tour Bus. Don't forget to bring your camera. We're going on vacation to Canada! Canada is one of the top ten tourism destinations in the world. What do tourists want to see when they come here? I'll show you the hot spots.

Destination Canada

Niagara Falls, in Ontario, are the best-known water-falls in the world. Over 12 million tourists come here each year. And have you ever seen so many gift shops?

Visit the home of Anne of Green Gables on Prince Edward Island. The book, by Canadian author Lucy Maud Montgomery, is a mega-hit in Japan, so you're bound to see busloads of Japanese tourists.

Put on your cowboy hat and boots, and head for the Calgary Stampede.

Ride the glass elevator to the top of the CN Tower in Toronto, the world's tallest freestanding structure!

This is not going to be good for my hat.

PRAY LAKE SAWMILLS

Look around—isn't this Rocky Mountain scenery mind-boggling? You can take a hike in Banff and Jasper national parks. Maybe you'll see bighorn sheep, mountain goats, elk, or (gulp!) grizzlies. Walk on the ancient ice of the Athabasca Glacier. That's so cool you might want to soak in the Banff hot springs afterwards.

Stay in a five-Star Ice Hotel! This hotel, just west of Quebec City, is the only one in North America made entirely of ice and snow. Inside temperature is -4°C (25°F). A unique Canadian experience! Don't delay; rooms book up a year in advance.

Visit the Bay of Fundy in New Brunswick to watch the world's highest tides roll up the beach.

Come to Canada's North, take a ride on a dogsled, and see the spectacular northern lights.

Questions Tourists Ask:

- Are there bears in Canada?....................Yes
- Can I feed the bears?...............................No
- Will I need a winter coat and snow boots in August?..No
- Can I pet the bears?.................................No
- Does "80 km/h" on the highway sign mean I can drive 80 miles an hour?.......No 80 km/h is the equivalent of 50 miles an hour. So, SLOW DOWN!
- Do I really have to wear a seat belt?...Yes
- Where's the washroom?

Souvenir of Canada

Secret agent Rachel (that's me) goes undercover posing as a tourist at a gift shop. There are gift shops at most big Canadian tourist attractions. My mission: to see what souvenirs of Canada are for sale. Time to go shopping!

Such clever Canadian moose! They paddle canoes, dress up like Mounties and lumberjacks, and skate on frozen ponds. (Canada's ponds are always frozen, of course.) Tourists find moose very cute—must be that big nose.

What could be more Canadian than hockey? Score a sale!

Hey—I should license moose souvenirs! That way I could get some of the money from them.

What would you do with the money? Visit the two places in Canada I've always wanted to see— Moosonee and Moosomin.

Mounties are a hot seller in the gift shop. (Those would be the red-coated Mounties on horseback bringing law and order to the Wild West! Not the ones that pull tourists over for speeding.) The RCMP has licensed all Mountie souvenirs. The money they receive helps fund RCMP programs such as Crime Stoppers and search and rescue.

Totem poles are not just funny animals standing on top of each other. The killer whales, eagles, thunderbirds, and other crests are full of symbolic meaning. Stories were passed down from one generation to the next through the totem poles.

Raarrrrrrr! Tourists love our wild beasts. They love the Canadian wilderness. You'd never know that most Canadians live in cities.

Tourists are fascinated by Indian souvenirs. Sometimes these totem poles, dream catchers, tomahawks, and other "authentic Indian souvenirs" are pretty silly. They show a Hollywood movie version of what Indians should look like. They may not have much to do with actual Native culture.

Canadians wear red plaid lumberjack shirts, eh? It's part of our northern image—we all live in log cabins in the bush, chopping down trees and hunting moose.

As Canadian as... maple syrup. Slurp it up!

Inuit souvenirs from the Romantic North are a big seller, too. You can buy inuksuk paperweights, dolls, stuffed polar bears, and cuddly huskies. You can also buy original artwork and sculptures by Inuit artists.

Dear reader: If you were going to pick one souvenir to represent Canada, what would you pick?

I would pick the moose playing hockey.

A good choice, Guy. Don't forget my fee.

87

So You Want to Be a Canadian?

Lucky me—I'm Canadian! Other people apparently think so. Over 200,000 people from other countries immigrate to Canada each year. Nearly 20 percent of Canadians have come from somewhere else. Many become Canadian citizens. Why do they come here? Definitely not because of the weather!

New Canadians have to learn about Canada. Some things that Canadians do may seem very strange to people from other countries.

(Note to Mrs. G: Don't get any ideas about becoming stricter!)

Reasons People Say They Come to Canada

- Canada is a peaceful country.
- Everyone here has equal rights. Women are treated as equal to men.
- Our children will have better opportunities here.
- I enjoy the wilderness.
- People are more tolerant here. There is less discrimination and racism.
- There's freedom of speech in Canada. We can say what we think, even if others disagree.
- Here, we can't be arrested and thrown in jail without a fair trial.
- I love the climate here!

My father was shocked at the lack of discipline in my school. He's used to a strict classroom, with students sitting in neat rows, in school uniforms, and teachers in total control.

Here's my story: I had just arrived in Canada. It was a dark and spooky night in late October. The doorbell rang. When I opened it, YIKES! There were devils and goblins at my door, and a ghost yelling, "Trick or Treat!" Nobody had told me about Hallowe'en.

I like it that most Canadians do not smoke. In other countries, many more people smoke. Here, a guest is expected to ask permission before lighting up a cigarette in your home. If you're a non-smoker, you might ask them to smoke outside.

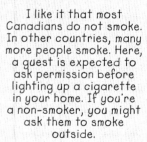

I found it odd to see Canadians take off their shoes when they enter their homes. At parties here, I sometimes see elegantly dressed people with no shoes on!

Canadian pooches like it when guests leave shoes at the door.

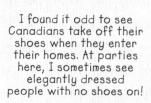

By the way, what are we lining up for?

I haven't a clue. I figured if I got in line, I'd eventually find out.

I find Canadians very orderly and courteous. They line up to wait their turn. They get mad if someone pushes ahead in a line-up.

The most amazing thing I found when I came to Canada was SNOW! Even my mother was excited about it. But by our third winter, like a typical Canadian, she was complaining about the weather.

Canadians are big on keeping their environment clean. Littering is not acceptable. People usually put their garbage into garbage cans. Many people recycle garbage. They even pick up after their dogs in the park!

I was amazed at the variety of people here! People of all colours, with different ethnic backgrounds, and many speaking foreign languages. But they're all Canadians! That blew me away!

The first time I went shopping for food in the supermarket, I got lost in the dog food section! Boy, those North American mega-stores are huge! I was used to buying food from small little shops. I also had to learn that Canadians don't try to bargain for a better price. Where I came from, bargaining is regular part of the shopping experience.

I can't believe how much Canadian kids complain because they have to go to school. Where I come from, attending school is a privilege, and only the luckiest get to go. Education is the only way to get out of poverty. I shake my head when I hear kids here griping about school.

I'm Canadian because... I talk about the weather. All the time.

Branding Canada:
EPISODE 3

WILL RETURN

Canada

Canada—
where the
good
times
flow.

I'm getting thirsty, Moose.
　　Probably because we've been thinking about
　　water, Goose. But you must admit, water
　　is a good brand image for Canada.
　Because we go from sea to sea!
　　A Mari usque ad Mare.
　If you say so. There's also lots of water in the middle.
　　Right. We have half of the world's fresh water
　　in our rivers and lakes.
And Niagara Falls!
　　A very well-known piece of Canadian water.
　　You've been there, haven't you, Goose?
　　Did you have a good time?
I sure did—it's where the good times flow.
　　Say that again?
It's where the good times flow.
　　Goose, you've got it!
　　"Canada—where the good times flow."
　It sounds inviting. It's a slogan we can put on
　pictures of our waterfalls, mountain streams,
　or anything, actually. It will remind people of
　all the clear, sparkling water that flows in Canada.
Glad to hear it! Gotta go now.
All that talk of flowing water...

Come on in!
The water's fine!

Canada—All Wet!

Glug, Glug Canada!

Thirsting after Canada?

Canada Awash! Afloat!
Flooded! Deluged! Sodden!

Canada:
Water You Waiting for?

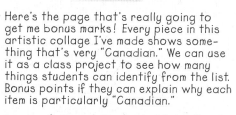

Here's the page that's really going to get me bonus marks! Every piece in this artistic collage I've made shows something that's very "Canadian." We can use it as a class project to see how many things students can identify from the list. Bonus points if they can explain why each item is particularly "Canadian."

List of Canadian stuff to find:

Bison
The Constitution
Birch bark canoe
Maple leaf
Maple syrup
Polar bear
Lacrosse stick
Caribou
Bucko Beaver
Inuksuk
Common loon
Loonie
Old bank note
Mountie
Poutine
Parliament Buildings
Fleur-de-lis
Queen Victoria
My rabbit
Baby moose
Anne of Green Gables
Husky dog
Grizzly bear
Gyrfalcon
Polar bear licence plate
French-English Sign
The Stanley Cup
Canadian flag
Saskatoon berries
Red River cart
Atlantic puffin
Provincial flags
Stuffed moose
Jacques Cartier

Hey, what's that lollipop doing in there?

92

I see a baby moose!

Anyone seen the maple syrup?

ANNE of GREEN GABLES
By L.M. MONTGOMERY

Canadian Pacific

Rach—you left glue all over the kitchen table! Better clean it up before Mom gets after you!

I can't! It's stuck on!

93

Acknowledgements

Rachel (a.k.a. Vivien) scoured the country to find fascinating facts for this book. Sometimes you have to dig for them. Thanks to the RCMP's Dave Hay who told her what kind of motorcycles the police ride; to the folks at Calgary Catholic Immigration Services who explained what new Canadian kids find strange about Canada; and to editor Anne Shone for discovering that people who study flags are called vexillologists (of course!). Thanks to the Ottawa gift shop owner who let Vivien take photos of his tacky souvenirs and to the Parliament Hill security guard who helped find her camera (turned out it was in her pocket all along—oops!). Thanks to Dianne Eastman for the zany, gorgeous illustrations for which Vivien gets undeserved compliments. Finally, kudos to the dedicated team at Maple Tree Press for believing that kids truly deserve wonderful books.

Photo Credits

Care has been taken to trace ownership of copyright materials contained in this book. Information enabling the publisher to rectify any reference or credit line in future editions will be welcomed.

For reasons of space, the following abbreviations have been used:

CMC: Canadian Museum of Civilization
GA: Glenbow Archives
HHOF: Hockey Hall of Fame
LOP: Library of Parliament/Bibliotheque du Parlement
NAC: National Archives of Canada
NCC: National Currency Collection, Currency Museum, Bank of Canada, photography Gord Carter, Ottawa.
RB: Robert Berdan
RSM: Royal Saskatchewan Museum
VB: Vivien Bowers
VP: Valan Photos

Page 9: LOP/Mone's Photography; 10: Théophile Hamel/NAC/C-041376; 11 (top): Jules I. Livernois/NAC/C-006350; 11 (middle right): courtesy Canadian Space Agency; 11 (bottom): Atomic Energy of Canada Ltd.; 12 (hats): NAC/C-17338; 12 (bottom): James. D. Markou/VP; 13 (top left): Toronto Reference Library/J. Ross Robertson Collection; 13 (bottom left): NCC; 13 (top right): Canadian Pacific Railway Archives/CPRL8; 13 (bottom right): NAC/POS-1759/©Canada Post Corporation, 1851, reproduced with permission; 14 (top left): Canada Science and Technology Museum/CN Collection/CN003804; 14 (bottom left): GA NA-3232; 14 (right): Courtesy of the Office of the Secretary to the Governor General; 15: *Canadian Illustrated News*, Vol. 1, No. 6, Page 93. Photo: From the National Library of Canada (http://www.imagescanada.ca/); 16: The Arms of Canada is reproduced with the permission of the Government of Canada; 18, 19: VB; 20 (top four, left to right): GA NA-684-1, NA-103~1, NA-1030, NA-1225; 20 (middle): Ken W. Watson, www.rideau-info.com; 20 (bottom): courtesy BeaverTails® Canada; 21: LOP/Mone's Photography; 22 (top right): LOP/W.J.L. Gibbons; 23 (top): LOP/Stephen Fenn; 23 (middle left): LOP/Doug Millar; 23 (middle right): LOP/Stephen Fenn; 24 (top): CMC, D-1776; 24 (middle, left to right): NA; 24 (bottom): National Film Board/NA/PA-165516; 25: courtesy Department of Canadian Heritage; 25 (bottom): VB; 26: with permission of House of Lords Record Office/NA/C-104073; 27 (top): with permission of the House of Lords Record Office/NA/C-104038; 27 (bottom left & right): VB; 29:

Doug MacLellan/HHOF; 30, 31: NCC; 32 (top): VB; 32 (current coins): Coin designs © courtesy of the Royal Canadian Mint/photography RB; 32 (12-sided nickel): NCC; 33 (current coins): Coin designs © courtesy of the Royal Canadian Mint/photography RB ; 33 (1937 dollar): NCC; 38 (flag & coat of arms): courtesy Province of British Columbia; 38 (page title): RB; 38 (licence plate): Insurance Corp. of British Columbia; 39: RB; 40 (flag & coat of arms): Courtesy Government of Alberta; 40 (page title): RB; 40 (licence plate): courtesy Alberta Government Services; 41 (top): Terry Parker/Ursus; 41 (upper middle): RB; 41 (old & new mace): courtesy Alberta Community Heritage Foundation; 41 (lower left): Terry Parker/Ursus; 41 (bottom): © Duane S. Radford; 42 (licence plate): Saskatchewan Government Insurance; 42 (flag & coat of arms): courtesy government of Saskatchewan; 42 (page title): Allen Lefebvre; 42 (bottom): RSM; 43 (top right & bottom left): RSM; 43 (top left & bottom right): Terry Parker/Ursus; 44 (flag ,coat of arms, & licence plate): courtesy Province of Manitoba; 44 (page title): Allen Lefebvre; 44 (bottom left): Terry Parker/UP; 44 (bottom right): courtesy Province of Manitoba; 45 (top): VB; 45 (bottom): courtesy Province of Manitoba; 46 (flag, coat of arms & trillium logo): courtesy Government of Ontario; 46 (page title): RB ; 46 (licence plate): courtesy Ministry of Transporation Ontario; 46 (trillium & loon): Ontario Tourism Marketing Partnership Corp.; 47: by TonyEno.com/Masquerader: Laverne More.; 48 (flag, licence plate, & coat of arms): courtesy Government of Quebec; 48 (page title): Francis Lépine/VP; 48 (bottom): Harold V. Green/VP; 49 (top): RB; 49 (middle): courtesy Government of Quebec; 49 (bottom): courtesy www.carnaval.qc.ca; 50 (flag & coat of arms): courtesy Government of New Brunswick/Communications New Brunswick; 50 (page title): courtesy Government of New Brunswick/Communications New Brunswick; 50 (licence plate): New Brunswick Department of Public Safety; 51: courtesy Government of New Brunswick/Communications New Brunswick; 52 (flag & coat of arms): Crown copyright Province of Nova Scotia. Reproduced with the permission of the Province of Nova Scotia; 52 (page title): John Fowler/VP; 52 (lower left): Jane Hugessen/VP; 52 (lower right): Roy Hamaguchi/UP; 52 (bottom): courtesy Government of Nova Scotia/Communications Nova Scotia; 53 (top right): Nova Scotia Museum, Natural History Collection, Halifax, Canada/Alex Wilson; 53 (upper right): Kennon Cooke/VP; 53 (middle): permission of Redpath Museum, McGill University; 53 (bottom): Francis Lépine/VP; 55 (flag & coat of arms): courtesy Government of Prince Edward Island; 54 (page title): V.Wilkinson/VP; 54 (licence plate):

courtesy Prince Edward Island Transportation and Public Works; 55 (top left): Stephen J. Krasemann/VP; 55 (top right): Robert C. Simpson/VP; 55 (lower left): Toronto Public Library/Osborne Collection of Early Children's Books; 56 (flag & coat of arms): courtesy Government of Newfoundland and Labrador; 56 (page title): Don Loveridge/VP; 56 (licence plate): courtesy Government Services & Lands, Provincial Government of Newfoundland and Labrador, Motor Registration Division; 57 (top left): courtesy Communications New Brunswick; 57 (top right): J.A. Wilkinson/VP; 57 (lower left): Aubrey Lang/VP; 57 (lower right): courtesy Communications New Brunswick; 57 (bottom): VB; 58 (flag, licence plate, & coat of arms): courtesy Government of Yukon Territory; 58 (page title): Stephen J. Krasemann/VP; 59 (top & upper left): RB; 59 (middle right): MacBride Museum (1989 1.1.120), Whitehorse, Yukon; 59 (bottom left): courtesy Canadian Tourism Commission; 60 (flag, coat of arms, & licence plate): courtesy Government of Northwest Territories; 60 (page title): Stephen J. Krasemann/VP; 61 (top right): Roy Tunami/Ursus; 61 (top left): John Eastcott/Yva Momatiuk/VP; 61 (upper right): © 2002 Phil Geusebroek; 61 (middle): Johnny Johnson/VP; 62 (flag, coat of arms, & licence plate): courtesy Government of Nunavut; 62 (page title): John Eastcott/Yva Momatiuk/VP; 63 (top left): Bruce Lyon/VP; 63 (top right & upper middle): Roy Tanami/Ursus; 63 (middle): Stephen J. Krasemann/VP; 63 (bottom left): Glen Williams/Ursus; 68 (upper right): HHOF; 68 (bottom): Dave Sandford/IIHF/HHOF; 68 ($1 coin): Coin designs © courtesy of the Royal Canadian Mint/photography RB; 69 (top left): Gretzky Family/HHOF; 69 (middle right): VB; 74 (top & middle): CMC (Dan Sarazin, 1970, Merle Toole, S96-24200); 74 (bottom): Ontario Tourism Marketing Parnership Corp.; 75 (top): Frances Anne Hopkins/NAC/-C-002774; 75 (bottom): courtesy www.carnaval.qc.ca; 78: RCMP -GRC; 79: © 2002 Her Majesty the Queen in Right of Canada as represented by the Solicitor General of Canada; 80 (middle right); courtesy Canadian Tourism Commission; 80 (bottom): RB; 81 (grizzly bear & caribou): Stephen J. Krasemann/VP; 81 (moose): RB; 81 (bottom): VB; 82: Stephen J. Krasemann/VP; 83: LOP/Mone's Photography; 84 (left): The Niagara Parks Commission; 84 (top right): courtesy Canadian Tourism Commission; 84 (bottom right): RB; 85 (top): RB; 85 (bottom left): Canadian Tourism Commission; 85 (bottom right): Kennon Cooke/VP.

Index

Alberta 40, 41
Aurora borealis (*see* Northern Lights)
Anne of Green Gables 55, 84
  Montgomery, Lucy, Maud 55

Birds
  atlantic puffin 57
  black-capped chickadee 51
  blue jay 54, 55
  great grey owl 44
  great horned owl 41
  gyrfalcon 61
  common loon 33, 46
  osprey 52
  raven 59
  rock ptarmigan 63
  sharp-tailed grouse 43
  snowy owl 49
  steller's jay 39
  willow ptarmigan 57
Bluenose (also *Bluenose II*) 32, 53
British Columbia 38, 39

Canadarm 11
CANDU (nuclear reactor) 11
Canoe 74, 75
Cartier, Jacques 10, 71
Currency 30–33

Explorers (European) 10, 12, 40, 71, 74

Festivals & Holidays
  Canada Day 83
  Remembrance Day 18
  Victoria Day 15
  Winter Carnival, Quebec City 49, 75
First Nations (aboriginal people) 12, 17, 19, 30, 74, 78
Fish
  bull trout 41
Flowers & plants
  blue flag 49
  fireweed 59
  fleur-de-lis 16, 48, 49
  lady's slipper 55
  mayflower 52
  mountain avens 61
  Pacific dogwood 38, 39
  pitcher plant 57
  purple saxifrage 63
  purple violet 51
  trillium 46
  western red lily 42, 43
  wild rose 40, 41

Food 42, 53, 72, 73
Fossils (*Hylonomus lyelli*) 53
France 16, 50
Fur trade 12, 13, 40, 75
  Hudson's Bay Company 31, 40
  Voyageurs 75

Geography 80
Gold Rush, Klondike 58, 81
Government
  Canadian Charter of Rights and Freedoms 27
  Canadian Constitution 26
  Confederation 11, 54
  House of Commons 9, 23
  Mace 9, 41
  Parliament Buildings 19, 21, 23
  Senate 23
  Governor general 14
  Queen Elizabeth II 14, 33
  Queen Victoria 14, 15
  Supreme Court of Canada 27
Great Britain 14, 16, 38, 50, 54, 71, 76, 77
  Red Ensign 24, 25
  Union Jack 16, 24, 38, 57

Immigrants 39, 42, 47
Immigration 88, 89
Insects 48, 81

Languages
  bilingual 10, 26, 50, 70, 71
  Chinese 39
  English 76, 77
  Francophones 70
  French 48
  Inuktitut 62

Mammals
  Arctic hare 61
  beaver 12, 13, 31, 32
  bison 45
  Canadian Inuit dog (*also* qummiq) 63
  caribou 33, 81
  duck tolling retriever 53
  grizzly bear 81
  moose 81
  Newfoundland dog 57
  Rocky Mountain bighorn sheep 41
  polar bear 33, 45, 81
  white-tailed deer 42, 43
  woolly mammoth 59
Manitoba 44, 45

National Emblems
  anthem 28, 29
  Coat of Arms 16
  flag 24, 25
  Great Seal of Canada 15
New Brunswick 50, 51
Newfoundland & Labrador 56, 57
Northern Lights 61
North Pole, the 63
North-West Mounted Police (*see* Royal Canadian Mounted Police)
Northwest Territories 60, 61
Nova Scotia 52, 53
Nunavut 62, 63

Ontario 46, 47
  Ottawa 9, 14, 18–21
  Niagara Falls 84

Prince Edward Island 54, 55

Quebec 48, 49
  Ice Hotel 85

Rocky Mountains 85
Royal Canadian Mounted Police (RCMP) 78, 79

Saskatchewan 42, 43
Service, Robert 59
Shipping & Shipbuilding 51
Sports
  curling 42
  hockey 68, 69

United Empire Loyalists 47, 50, 71
United States (of America) 76, 77, 82, 83
Upper/Lower Canada 10

World War I 18
World War II 32

Yukon 58, 59

Wow! Rachel should write a sequel to this book.
Or make it the first of a trilogy.
I see film potential: "That's Very Canadian—the movie!"

Could we have Bucko Beaver
action figures?